HOT
OFF
THE
PRESS

HOT OFF THE PRESS

PRINTS & POLITICS

EDITED BY LINDA TYLER AND BARRY WALKER

PUBLISHED FOR TAMARIND INSTITUTE BY

THE UNIVERSITY OF NEW MEXICO PRESS ALBUQUERQUE

Copyright © 1994 by Tamarind Institute.
FIRST EDITION
Library of Congress Cataloging-in-Publication Data
Hot off the press : prints and politics / edited by Linda
Tyler and Barry Walker. — 1st ed.
p.   cm.
ISBN 0-8263-1496-1
1. Politics in art.   2. Social problems in art.
3. Prints—Themes, motives.   I. Tyler, Linda.
II. Tamarind Institute.
NE962.P64H68   1994
760'.1—dc20   93-5600
                                              CIP

Volume Fifteen of *The Tamarind Papers* is the first of a
biennial series to be published by the University of
New Mexico Press. Semiannual through biennial
Volumes One through Fourteen, published between
1974 and 1993, are available from:
    Tamarind Institute
    108 Cornell Drive, SE
    Albuquerque, NM 87106

CONTENTS

PREFACE

This fifteenth volume of *The Tamarind Papers,* in its proud new format, is the first to be published by the University of New Mexico. It heralds a new tangent to the tradition begun by Tamarind Director Emeritus Clinton Adams in 1974. From twelve pages of technical writings that made up Volume One, *TTP* evolved under Adams's editorship into a full-fledged journal of historical, critical, and technical articles that covered diverse, yet related, topics of interest to the print connoisseur as well as to the printer, the curator, the artist, and the historian. Adams's last issue as full-time editor in 1990 celebrated the thirtieth anniversary of Tamarind's presence with *Perspectives and Reappraisals,* a concise review of printmaking highlights from 1960 through 1990.

With his move to the editorial board, Adams helped to see *TTP* through a smooth transition to its current position by suggesting noted British curator and scholar Pat Gilmour as *TTP*'s first guest editor. Just as Gilmour gathered new perspectives and reappraisals for her Volume Fourteen focus on avant-garde British printmaking, other guest editors with specialized interests would ensure the continuance of this journal's dedication to the fine print.

Barry Walker, curator of prints and drawings at the Museum of Fine Arts in Houston, Texas, lends as guest editor of this volume the curatorial eye that directed three Brooklyn Museum national print exhibitions. Nine writers examine for us aspects of more than five hundred years of social and political prints and printmaking. Walker himself contributes an interview with Eric Avery, whose unbound linocut *Heartland Hate Summit,* printed at Tamarind by Master Printer Bill Lagattuta on pages from the United States Budget Report, is included in this volume. Avery's large-edition print embodies the artist's philosophical stance about printmaking as it reflects twentieth-century social and political concerns in the manner of the widely disseminated fifteenth- and sixteenth-century "visual message" woodcut prints. The skeletal figure of death in many of Avery's prints recalls the death figures of prints such as Marchant's 1490 woodcuts in *La danse macabre—* the "ferocious satires of Death the Leveler that anticipate the *ça ira* of the French Revolution." *

Stephen Pinson chooses the French Revolution as a backdrop for his essay about prints,

*A. Hyatt Mayor, *Prints and People: A Social History of Printed Pictures* (New York: The Metropolitan Museum of Art, 1971), illustration 54.

politics, and the emergence of modernism in nineteenth-century France. In writing about "the near-caricature" of Charlet's *Le marchand de dessins lithographiques* of 1819, whose soldier ironically "would soon become a popular icon thanks to the phenomenon of political caricature," Pinson propels us to America and to the decade Peter Walch calls "the heroic 1930s." With his essay on the American League Against War and Fascism 1936 Calendar, Walch joins Ellen Sragow and Reba White Williams in examining this important printmaking period. Sragow revives the WPA days of Harry Gottlieb and Gustave von Groschwitz, and Williams enhances her essay on Robert Gwathmey with the first illustrated and annotated checklist of his prints.

Lynne Allen's conversations with Leon Golub and Nancy Spero reveal contemporary artists who "individually target many aspects of a diseased twentieth-century society while searching for a fundamental self." Clinton Adams interviews artist Patrick Nagatani about his "contextually loaded" waterless planographs produced with Tamarind Master Printer Jeffrey Ryan at 21 Steps workshop. Ryan follows with thoughts about the aesthetic impact of prints produced by this method, after which 1993 Tamarind Master Printer Veda Ozelle describes step-by-step her research into "siligraphy," or waterless lithography. Mark Petr, a curatorial assistant at Houston's Museum of Fine Arts, provokes new considerations of the engagement of printmaking with critical theory in his essay "Prints, Politics, Polemics."

It is the collaborative spirit that especially distinguishes this volume. The efforts of these fine writers and our enthusiastic reception from UNM Press signify to us a much-appreciated tribute to *TTP*'s reputation as well as an acknowledgment of shared standards of excellence. We also appreciate the financial and philosophical support of UNM's Office of Associate Provost for Research. To the end of living up to these confidences placed in us, we pledge our continued efforts toward the standard established by Clinton Adams as we continue to report on historical, critical, and technical issues in printmaking. As always, we welcome your comments and suggestions.

Linda Tyler
TAMARIND INSTITUTE

HOT OFF THE PRESS

GUSTAVE VON GROSCHWITZ

Historian, Curator, Lover of Lithography and All That Mattered

Ellen Sragow

Gustave von Groschwitz died on August 11, 1991, at eighty-five, only a few weeks after the death of his dear wife Fran, at eighty-four, on July 15.

"Von," as he was affectionately known by his friends, colleagues, and family, and Fran were inseparable. During their marriage of over fifty-eight years, they remained college sweethearts. They were always ready to attend openings, exhibitions, and symposia having to do with prints, especially lithographs. Von would arrive in a suit and tie, and you could always count on Fran to appear in a wonderful, brightly colored dress with a special hat and high-heeled shoes! They were the personification of dignity and charm.

Although he had retired from curatorial positions, Von never stopped working. He was constantly approached to write articles, participate in symposia, and comment on the state of the art of lithography and the print world in general. He was always available and eager to answer questions by interested students and professionals in the field. Von was very modest and, if you praised his expertise or showed admiration, he usually accepted it by paying you an enormous compliment as well.

Gustave von Groschwitz had an enthusiasm for prints that began during his student days at Columbia College, where he studied with artist/printmaker Albert Heckman. He graduated in 1926, two months after his twentieth birthday. From 1935 to 1938, he was supervisor of the Graphic Arts Division of the Federal Art Project in New York. Along with many of the artists on the project, he was very interested in lithography and encouraged them to experiment with color lithography. Prior to the WPA, artists had been limited to making mostly black-and-white images, due to the high costs of creating prints at professional workshops.

In 1937 the Federal Art Gallery on Fifty-seventh Street in New York City exhibited only 4 color lithographs in a print show of WPA graphics. In 1938 there were 23, and, by 1942, there were 134, created by forty-seven artists, including Harry Gottlieb. These color lithographs are in the collection of the Metropolitan Museum of Art.

Von spoke fondly of his experiences on the WPA during a symposium in 1989 at Lehman College. He felt that "the experience on the project was the nearest to heaven that I have met so far."[1] At another symposium, in 1985, he was able to reminisce about those wonderful days. He was invited to participate in a panel discussion on the WPA (coordinated by Ellen Sragow), sponsored by the Mitchell Wolfson, Jr., Collection of Decorative and Propaganda Arts in Miami,

Florida. This was a great reunion for him, with the opportunity to meet with several artists he had not seen for almost fifty years! He commented that "looking back about a century we see that the color lithography unit served as a link between the great lithographers in Paris during the 1890s and the American revival of the 1950s which culminated in the superb color lithographs of Jasper Johns, Jim Dine, Nathan Olivera, and others."[2]

After the WPA Project, Von became Curator of Prints at Wesleyan University. He received his master's degree in art history in 1949 from the Institute of Fine Arts, New York University, writing his thesis on nineteenth-century color lithography.

In 1947 Von became curator of prints at the Cincinnati Art Museum and remained there until 1963. During those years he was devoted to color lithography. In 1950 he organized the First International Biennial of Contemporary Color Lithography, at the Cincinnati Art Museum. This was the first of five exhibitions held every other year. During those years he was able to purchase color lithographs by Vuillard, Bonnard, and others for as little as $150 per print! He built one of the finest collections of nineteenth- and twentieth-century lithographs in the country.

These biennials influenced the revival of the medium of color lithography throughout the United States. In 1960 its name was changed to the International Biennial of Prints and included prints in all media.

2.2 Théodore Géricault, *Le maréchal français*, from *Etudes de chevaux*, 1822. Lithograph. 41.9 × 55.2 cm.

ture, these prints elevated what had been a narrow genre into the dignified and poetical, through the new and association-free medium of lithography. Unfortunately, given the rapid pace of artistic change, Géricault's prints did not find the audience he had hoped for, and his art did not affect lithographic practice in France until many years after his death.[3]

Instead, much imagery was controlled by the regime in power, as artists continued to produce political propaganda in the guise of "high" art. From the massive revolt of 1789, the French citizenry had inherited a canon of gestures that cried out for pictorial expression, and many artists responded by creating what can be thought of as the "revolutionary image." These idealized, sometimes Romantic pictures represented the revolution's new philosophical and political ideas, as well as its new leaders and heroes. This political ethos ran especially high under the reign of Napoléon I, when such imagery typically conveyed more myth than reality. Bourgeois de la Richardière's idealized *Napoléon, premier consul*

2.3 Bourgeois de la Richardière, *Napoléon, first consul*, ca. 1802. Stipple engraving with etching, 42.5 × 30.8 cm.

2.4 Nicolas-Toussaint Charlet, *French Dragoon with a Flag,* n.d. Lithograph. 54.0 × 32.9 cm.

(figure 2.3), for example, approaches the realm of allegory through the use of imperial iconography.

The graphic arts, due to their reproductive capacity and ease of dissemination, were perfectly suited to bring such benign renderings of Napoléon and other political "men of the hour" to *le peuple,* or the French lower classes. And with the rise of illustrated books and popular journals, the revolutionary image was transformed into an even more generalized type of art. This change is evidenced in the work of Nicolas-Toussaint Charlet, from the heroic *French Dragoon with a Flag* (figure 2.4), to the near caricature of *Le marchand de dessins lithographiques* (figure 2.5). In the latter print, Charlet predicts the shape of things to come with his "deromanticized" soldier perusing a collection of popular prints; the irony, of course, is that the soldier himself would soon become a popular icon, thanks to the phenomenon of political caricature.

Charles Philipon launched the weekly journal *La Caricature* in 1830, during a brief relaxation of press laws at the beginning of Louis-Philippe's self-proclaimed "liberal" reign. Within the pages of this journal, and later in the daily *Le Charivari,* Honoré Daumier reinvented the revolutionary image of Romanticism, turning it upside down, inside out, and finally casting it before the eyes of a newly perceptive French republic. In *Moderne Galilée* (figure 2.6), for example, Daumier depicts a jailed pressman stoically facing the chief prosecutor of Louis-Philippe. Above the two men, the

well-known figure of Liberty (used to such different effect only four years earlier by Delacroix) illumines the many years of struggle against increasingly abusive regimes. Worlds apart from Delacroix's allegory, Daumier's art is an early manifestation, in full force by midcentury, of a profound artistic and intellectual disillusionment with the experience of revolution.

CARICATURE AND THE COLLAPSE OF REVOLUTIONARY MYTH

The initial uprising of February 1848 had ended the reign of Louis-Philippe, created a provisional government, and renewed the hope for reform. For a time people believed that the alliance that had briefly linked bourgeois and worker in 1830 had become permanent. By June, however, fear of what was thought to be a growing radical element among the workers had greatly weakened political allegiances. With the brutal defeat of the insurgents came the notion that the revolutionary polemics of the 1790s were no longer valid. An article from *Le National* on June 29, 1848, included the following: "Deceived by false appearances, led astray by promises that will not be kept, how many good men have perhaps already paid for their cruel mistakes with their lives?" [4] The French state, having reached a formal crisis, was going through a process of redefinition.

Of course different individuals had different reasons for reacting against the ideals of the original revolution, but an unfavorable reaction was pervasive. Within the space of three years, for example, the socialist philosopher Pierre-Joseph Proudhon exchanged his hopeful revolutionary zeal for a despairing view of France under Louis-Napoléon. After being imprisoned in June of 1849 for criticism of the new regime, Proudhon formulated his political objective in *L'idée générale de la révolution au XIXe siècle:* "Let us work for the future. Let us picture the revolution. It will happen when it can. All the same we must be aware of it, if we want it to occur." By November of 1852, after almost a year of Louis-Napoléon's self-proclaimed empire, he was no longer so hopeful: "The specious and bourgeois reaction grows increasingly acute under the authority of Louis-Napoléon. Increasingly tyrannical conduct. Mutual fear, division, hatred, silence, this is France." [5]

Hatred and fear leading to silence and division: the sense of disillusionment is overpowingly apparent. Such changes in attitude were common among artists and writers during this period. These people had experienced a fundamental shift in their understanding of French society. Having grown up in the shadow of the legends of 1789, these individuals lived in constant anticipation of the society that had been promised to them. In the course of the political uprisings that plagued France in the nineteenth century, however, they began to question the rhetoric and ideology that had compelled their belief in the myth of revolution. This attitude's pervasiveness is evidenced by the writings of disparate thinkers, who all came to share a reactionary stance toward the revolutionary polemics of the 1790s.

2.5 Nicolas-Toussaint Charlet, *Le marchand de dessins lithographiques* (The lithograph seller), 1819. Lithograph, 28.6 × 38.6 cm.

2.6 Honoré Daumier, *Moderne Galilée,* from *La Caricature,* 1834. Lithograph, 27 × 36.5 cm.

In his writings on the eighteenth Brumaire of Louis-Napoléon Bonaparte, Karl Marx identified and criticized the anachronistic spell of the revolutionary myth:

> Hegel remarks somewhere that all facts and personages of great importance in world history occur, as it were, twice. He forgot to add: the first time as tragedy, the second as farce. Caussidière for Danton, Louis-Blanc for Robespierre, the Montagne of 1848–1851 for the Montagne of 1793–1795, the Nephew for the Uncle. And the same caricature occurs in the circumstances attending the second edition of the eighteenth Brumaire![6]

Marx's view, tinged with irony and sarcasm, is the most familiar and possibly the most important symptom of this reaction toward the failure of Romantic thought. Marxism and its progeny, Social Realism, gave rise to an ideology—sometimes pseudointellectual but always powerful—that still affects our understanding of art, culture, politics, and the history of ideas. Yet Marxism was, in its time, only a symptom of a larger cause. And it was not alone.

In *Recollections* of the 1848 uprising, Alexis de Tocqueville's description of the February invasion of the National Assembly echoed Marx's criticism of the eighteenth Brumaire. The myth of revolution has reduced the rebels to unwitting agents in a social travesty: "The whole time, I had the feeling that we had staged a play about the French Revolution, rather than that we were continuing it."[7] This recognition disturbed Tocqueville even to a greater extent than it did Marx, because he considered himself a victim of political rhetoric. He came to view the latest revolution as part of an endless series begun in 1789, with each successive uprising looking back to the original, cultivating the various myths produced by 1789 and 1793 and complicating them with latter-day variations. "I am tired," he wrote, "of mistaking deceptive mists for the bank. And I often wonder whether the solid land we have sought for so long actually exists, and whether it is not our fate to rove the seas forever!"[8]

Tocqueville's first reaction, much like that of caricature artists, was to deal in comic terms with his own sense of disillusionment. In order to criticize the actions of the people in the raid on the National Assembly, Tocqueville compared them to actors in a "vile tragedy played by a provincial troupe."[9] He poked fun at the president running frightened from the platform: "Never would I have believed that fear could accelerate such a fat body so much or, rather, suddenly transmogrify it into a sort of liquid."[10] Using vivid imagery, Tocqueville employed rather conventional (that is, Romantic and allegorical) language to criticize the myth of revolution.

This semantic trap, in which the opposition finds itself employing the language of its adversary, is a common occurrence in virtually all cultural struggles. And, as Richard Terdiman points out, it played an especially significant role in nineteenth-century France, where language itself became contested terrain.[11] In the course of the successive political and social struggles that helped to create modern France, writers constantly sought to produce new modes and styles that would set their work apart from officially sanctioned, historically accepted forms. Artists found themselves in a similar struggle, realizing that as long as they engaged the structure of revolutionary imagery, they were helping to uphold and even propagate the myth of revolution—a myth that blinded people (like Tocqueville) to reality by enslaving them to past ideals.

Daumier was possibly the first artist to realize the irony of this situation, and his oeuvre reveals a steady progression away from allegory, as well as from the generalized "types" of Romantic idealism. *Rue Transnonain, le 15 avril 1834* (figure 2.7) is an early and brilliant example of this move toward a new realism. In what is probably his most famous lithograph, Daumier unflinchingly unveils the horrific aftermath of the suppression of a silk workers' strike in Lyons and announces a new language in the representation of revolution.

After confronting his own sense of disenchantment, Tocqueville employed this new language to describe the June days of 1848. His descrip-

2.7 Honoré Daumier, *Rue Transnonain, le 15 avril 1834*. Lithograph. 21.6 × 31.7 cm.

tion, however horrible the subject matter, remains matter-of-fact and emotionally detached:

On my way back in the rue des Jeûneurs, I met a member of the National Guard covered with blood and bits of brain; he was very pale and on the way home. I asked him what was happening; he told me that his battalion had just been facing very murderous fire at point-blank range at the Saint-Denis gate; one of his comrades, whose name he told me, had been killed by his side, and it was that unlucky man's blood and brains with which he was spattered.[12]

Tocqueville renders the effects of the uprising through the experience of one soldier, bringing the reader face to face with the reality of the June days. This dramatic change in the conception of revolution, with its detailed depiction of the visual traces of violence, is also apparent in more popular forms of literature. After witnessing the aftermath of the 1848 revolt, for example, the protagonist of Gustave Flaubert's *Sentimental Education* becomes conscious of the idealistic myths that typify the "artificial world in which he suffered so much."[13] And Victor Hugo, in a passage from *Souvenirs personnels,* describes a scene at the barricades in which two young prostitutes expose themselves to members of the National Guard, daring them to shoot. Both of the girls are killed, one after the other.[14] In assuming the guise of a common whore, Liberty

is forcefully brought up to date, where political rhetoric must accommodate the uncertainties and ambiguities of modern life.

REVOLUTIONIZING THE REAL: THE POLITICS OF DISAFFECTION

Abundant evidence points to the midcentury rejection of revolutionary myth. However, many critics argue that artists after 1848 had simply come to ignore, or were unable to deal with, France's political atmosphere, which had driven many artists, such as Millet, to Barbizon. There the new spirit of Realism signified a critical change in subject matter, as artists turned from historical scenes and portraiture to rural peasant life and landscapes. Daily reality, however resistant it might have been to aesthetic uses, was in the process of becoming a viable subject for art.

Although some critics explain this apparent waning of political themes as the result of censorship and stylistic changes, other critics instead see the failure of an emerging nineteenth-century modernism.[15] This latter viewpoint became especially prominent with the rise of social history in the late 1960s, when a new wave of critics began forcing art—in an unprecedented manner—to serve their own ideological agendas.[16] Marxist,

2.8 Maxime Lalanne, *Démolitions pour le percement de la rue des Ecoles,* n.d. Etching with chine collé, 34.6 × 48.3 cm.

feminist, and French poststructuralist critics, each offering distinct interpretations, nevertheless maintained one essential point: art is always political and is only meaningful when serving a social purpose.

In *The Absolute Bourgeois,* for instance, T. J. Clark maintains that after June of 1848, artists found it increasingly difficult to produce public images of revolution. Increased violence and fear had produced political confusion that in turn, writes Clark, "bred aesthetic confusion."[17] As a result artists working from 1848 on were only able to deal with the revolution in "various disguises."[18] Clark cites Millet's toiling forest workers and Daumier's saltimbanques as examples of social groups left behind by economic progress after the 1850s. While such efforts evidence active endorsement of the politics of revolution, Clark believes that due to the indirect nature of their artistic expression, these artists were not entirely successful. The problem, writes Clark, "was to discover the point at which public and private intersect, and thus be able to attack one by depicting the other. The artist had to begin so it seemed, with an image of private life, since the forms of public existence were too chaotic and windblown for depiction."[19]

In *The Painting of Modern Life,* Clark even goes so far as to say that "modern" artists, in this case the nineteenth-century avant-garde, generally failed to respond to the social and political issues of their time. In particular Clark criticizes the ideology of these artists, whom he charges with overlooking the role of class struggle in modern life: "The avant-garde appears to have been persuaded by the view that modernity was no longer characterized by a system of classification and control but, rather, by mixture, transgression, and ambiguity in the general conduct of life."[20]

Did the disintegration of the revolutionary image after 1848, then, depend mainly upon artists' inability to deal with the transformations of class tensions and the rise of capitalism during the reign of Louis-Napoléon? Paris, transformed by Baron Haussmann from a medieval to a modern city, certainly did undergo major changes during this period. And while the destruction of slums made poverty more apparent and even drove a majority of the working class outside the boundaries of the city, the segregation of the classes does not seem to have been a major result of the renovation. In fact Donald Olsen argues that antagonism between the classes was present before the renovation and that "the serious contemporary criticisms that Haussmann faced were not that his policies produced socially segregated neighborhoods, but that they were bankrupting the city and the state."[21]

In another opposing view, Marshall Berman states that "fluidity and vaporousness" were the primary components of late-nineteenth-century modernism and that these traits were stimulated by Haussmann's opening of the city: "[He] opened up the whole of the city, for the first time in its history, to all of its inhabitants . . . Now, after centuries of life as a cluster of isolated cells, Paris was becoming a unified physical and human space."[22] So while the concept of class remained an issue in modern society, there is little evidence to indicate that artists were failing to respond to an overwhelming increase in segregation.

This does not mean, however, that artists suddenly extracted themselves from social and political discourse. The realistic visualization of the ongoing process of change registers instead as an awareness of the increasing gap between political idealism and political reality. Take for example Maxime Lalanne's arresting *Démolitions pour le percement de la Rue des Écoles* (figure 2.8), from an album chronicling Haussmann's renovation of Paris. Lalanne's print concentrates on the theme of destruction in the name of progress, while hinting at a movement away from figuration into the realm of abstraction. In this sense the intricate patterns created by the demolished buildings can even be seen as fitting symbols for the collapse of revolutionary myth and the birth of modern art.

This concentration on surface reality (and consequently on the surface of the work of art itself, a quality inherent in all Modernist modes) reverberated throughout all the emerging aesthetic languages of the nineteenth century. Daumier's later work relies less on exaggerated distortion and more on representational verity.[23] Millet's monumental peasants can be read as precursors to Cézanne and even as pre-Cubist portraits.[24] Charles Meryon, in deeply personal and often disturbing etchings, replaces myth and allegory with near fantasy, populating the streets and skies of the modern city with strange creatures (see, for example, the mourning figure in *Le Morgue,* figure 2.9). "And this movement, by which 'realism' is imagined to achieve something like the effect of a penetratingly corrosive surreal, becomes a technique for opening up contemporary social existence from the inside," where artists could

2.9 Charles Meryon, *La morgue,* 1854. Etching, 48 × 32.4 cm.

loudly proclaim their estrangement from modern society.[25]

Thus we see Meryon's etched fantasies as more than just the reveries of a troubled mind. Meryon, representing the epitome of nineteenth-century disaffection, truly stood at the critical juncture of Realism and the many modes of Modernism. On an intensely personal aesthetic quest, he explored the boundaries between reality and unreality, formalism and abstraction, thereby opening the psychological Pandora's box that would come to haunt many artists after him. An artist increasingly alone with his art, Meryon did intuitively, and with obvious pain, what Vuillard, Toulouse-Lautrec, Jacques Villon, and other masters would later do ever more deliberately, ever more consciously, assuring not merely the continued aesthetic interest, but the social primacy of French graphic arts. And finally, in his lifelong retreat from reality, Meryon irrevocably revealed the full palette of modernist themes and questions explored by artists through the nineteenth century and beyond.

Like Tocqueville and Flaubert, artists after the middle of the century purposefully distanced themselves from Romantic and revolutionary language, signs, and symbols. Tocqueville presented an objective view of the 1848 revolution to warn of the abuses of language and ideas that are possible when people become blinded by an abstract principle. Artists like Manet must have had similar goals. By dismantling the myth of the barricades, he moved one step closer to revealing the dangers in the abuses of the myth of revolution. And these dangers, as Flaubert wrote in 1869, were quite real. Well-versed in the Romantic and idealistic view of revolution, the French people were not prepared for the outcome of the 1848 uprising:

> Equality—as if to punish its defenders and ridicule its enemies—asserted itself triumphantly: an equality of brute beasts, a common level of bloody atrocities; for the fanaticism of the rich counterbalanced the frenzy of the poor, the aristocracy shared the fury of the rabble, and the cotton nightcap was just as savage as the red bonnet. The public's reason was deranged as if by some great natural upheaval. Intelligent men lost their sanity for the rest of their lives.[26]

The art of "modern life" portrayed a shifting and uncertain world, where uncomfortable reality was increasingly substituted for the myths of contemporary society. Regardless of whether this precluded specific representations of class, it certainly did not preclude the artist's feeling of increased alienation in a society stripped of its ideals. This alienation, viewed for too long as social failure or an aesthetic snubbing of things political, raises questions not only of meaning but also of methodology—should history be forced to bear the fruit of current ideological agendas? As Charles Harrison succinctly states in his recent incisive review of Michael Fried's *Courbet's Realism:* "For all our supposed Postmodernism, it seems that we are left with a form of the familiar question. To what extent can these projects be made to converge: the critique of art that is based on an understanding of historical process, and the understanding of historical process that is formed by the critical experience of art?"[27]

NOTES

Portions of this essay appeared in the exhibition guide accompanying *Political Aesthetics: From the Revolutionary Image to Modernism in Nineteenth-Century French Prints* at the Archer M. Huntington Art Gallery, the University of Texas at Austin (June 29–August 12, 1990). The exhibition was organized and presented in partial fulfillment of a thesis project in the Humanities Program of the College of Liberal Arts at the University of Texas. I gratefully acknowledge the advice and support of Professor Donald Aynesworth, Department of French and Italian, and Jonathan Bober, curator of prints and drawings, Archer M. Huntington Art Gallery. And for her consummate editorial skill, I thank Amy Root.

1. Helen G. Gardner, *Art Through the Ages* (New York: Harcourt, Brace, 1948), 675.

2. Charles Rosen and Henri Zerner, *Romanticism and Realism: The Mythology of Nineteenth-Century Art* (New York: Viking Press, 1984), 1–37.

3. A. Hyatt Mayor, *Prints and People* (New York: Metropolitan Museum of Art, 1971), 618.

4. Reprinted in *1848 in France,* ed. by Roger Price, part of the series *Documents of Revolution,* Heinz Lubasz, general editor (Ithaca and London: Cornell University Press, 1975), 116.

5. Pierre-Joseph Proudhon, *Oeuvres complètes,* nouvelle édition, publiée avec des notes et des documents inédits, C. Bougle et H. Moysset (Paris: M. Rivièrre, 1923).

6. Karl Marx, *The Eighteenth Brumaire of Louis Bonaparte* (New York: International Publishers, 1926), 15.

7. Alexis de Tocqueville, *Recollections* (New York: Columbia University Press, 1949), 53.

8. Ibid., 66.

9. Ibid., 53.

10. Ibid., 52.

11. Richard Terdiman, *Discourse/Counter-Discourse: The Theory and Practice of Symbolic Resistance in Nineteenth-Century France* (Ithaca and London: Cornell University Press, 1985), 43. Terdiman deals with problems of cultural struggle mostly in terms of literature, but includes a particularly insightful chapter on satirical journals and the art of Daumier.

12. Tocqueville, *Recollections,* 139.

13. Gustave Flaubert, *Sentimental Education* (London: Dent, 1964), 302.

14. Victor Hugo, *Souvenirs personnels* (Paris: Gallimard, 1952).

15. See, for example, Stuart Kadison, "The Politics of Censorship," in Beatrice Farwell, ed., *The Charged Image: French Lithographic Caricature 1816–1848* (Santa Barbara: Santa Barbara Museum of Art, 1989), 23–27: "Caricature thereafter [after the suspension of *La Caricature* in 1842] . . . confined itself to entertaining, but largely innocuous, social comment on the customs of the day. As in another celebrated caricature by Daumier, *Baissez le rideau, la farce est jouée,* the curtain had fallen. The heroic era of political caricature had come to an end."

16. See Robert Darnton's essay "Intellectual and Cultural History," in his book *The Kiss of Lamourette: Reflections in Cultural History* (New York and London: Norton, 1990), 191–218. Using data collected between 1948 and 1978 from eight major American universities, Darnton carefully charts the expansion of articles,

courses, and dissertations in social history, by which he means history based on techniques borrowed from demography, economics, and sociology, as opposed to intellectual history, by which he means the history of ideas.

17. T. J. Clark, *The Absolute Bourgeois: Artists and Politics in France, 1848–1851* (London: Thames and Hudson, 1973), 56.

18. Ibid., 71.

19. Ibid., 181.

20. T. J. Clark, The Painting of Modern Life: Paris in the Art of Manet and His Followers (New York: Knopf, 1985), 258.

21. Donald Olsen, *The City as a Work of Art: London, Paris, Vienna* (New Haven: Yale University Press, 1986), 143.

22. Marshall Berman, *All That is Solid Melts into Air* (New York: Simon and Schuster, 1982), 150–51.

23. Terdiman, *Discourse,* 196: "Daumier was reaching for something new, toward a subtler expressive system, one whose corrosion was more infrastructural. Thus with the post-Macaire depictions of the middle class, his drawings (and indeed their captions) increasingly attain effects which are based on strikingly different and, I will argue, more modern protocols of representation. They seek to achieve their deconstruction of the figures depicted not so much by an immediately recognizable *distortion* of their physiognomies or their reported speech but by a selection of referents for representation which locates the critique not in the manner of their deformation *but in their surface reality itself.*" (Terdiman's emphasis)

24. Mayor, *Prints,* 674.

25. Terdiman, *Discourse,* 197.

26. Flaubert, *Sentimental Education,* 334.

27. Charles Harrison, in a review of Michael Fried's *Courbet's Realism,* in *The Art Bulletin* (June 1992), 74(2):344.

THE AMERICAN LEAGUE AGAINST WAR AND FASCISM 1936 CALENDAR

Peter Walch

Ah, the heroic 1930s! Of all the periods in which American art has turned distinctly political, the decade of the Great Depression certainly ranks preeminent for the quality, quantity, and distinctive style of much of the art then produced.

It also does not hurt that many artists— politically engaged artists—of the thirties were powerful polemicists. And the graphic arts were especially favored both in deed and in word. According to muralist and printmaker Harry Sternberg:

> The graphic arts have a special importance for the growing numbers of artists anxious to turn their talents to the service of the struggle against War and Fascism. No other medium has the adaptability of the print, which can be produced rapidly and inexpensively in large quantities, and can be distributed at low cost.[1]

Illustrator and art director John Groth:

> That many fine artists have deliberately chosen their own ivory towers rather than subject themselves to momentary discomforts in the commercial field is

regrettable. Genius under a bushel basket is not so important as bare talent which finds its way into thousands of homes.[2]

Printmaker Louis Lozowick:

Nothing could be more sterile than exclusive pre-occupation with technical experimentation, and nothing more foreign to the best traditions of the graphic artists. This is especially important to remember now, when progress and reaction are contending throughout the world. The integrity of the artist and the very fate of art are threatened today. If the artist fastens the attention of his contemporaries on a living issue, he continues in the present the work of the great graphic artists of the past.[3]

Artist and arts organizer Ralph Pearson:

The artist ceases to be an ornament of the pink-tea, a playboy companion of the dilettante patron, a remote hero with a famous name. He becomes, instead, a workman among workers. He prints his etchings, lithographs or woodblocks with hands which know ink and the rollers and wheels of his press. He works. He produces. He lives.[4]

The enemy was the limited-edition print: in Harry Sternberg's words, "a pretentious front for speculation with an artificially limited product." Numerous artists, especially left-leaning artists, participated in "democratic-print" projects, often featuring unlimited runs of offset-printed litho-graphs, and often produced as fundraisers for causes on the Left.

One such project was the 1936 calendar, featuring the work of twelve different artists, printed and sold by the American League Against War and Fascism.[5] Like many another cause of the thirties, the American League Against War and Fascism is now little remembered. Computerized searches at several research libraries kept coming up with the unhelpful suggestion that maybe I really wanted "American League, Baseball." In its own day, however, the American League Against War and Fascism was one of the largest, most prominent, and most broadly based popular organizations on the Left.

Formed in 1933 following an August 1932 international antiwar congress in Amsterdam, it was one of forty-three national units of a World Committee Against War and Fascism. Dr. Harry F. Ward of the Union Theological Seminary was the league's second and longest-serving president. Prominent members included the authors Sherwood Anderson, Theodore Dreiser, and Upton Sinclair, the feminist Harriot Stanton Blatch, Communist party general secretary Earl Browder, and NAACP field secretary William Pickens. The pages of the league's monthly magazine, *Fight Against War and Fascism,* regularly featured the artwork of William Gropper, Harry Sternberg, Art Young, and Moses Soyer. The league survived a name change (in 1936, to "American League for

3.2 A. Redfield, illustration for American League Against War and Fascism calendar, 1936, one page of twelve.

Peace and Democracy"), but collapsed after the outbreak of war in 1939.

Looking at the 1936 calendar today, we find images by the famous, the not-quite-so-famous, and the positively obscure. Adolf Dehn (June), William Gropper (December), Louis Lozowick (November), and Louis Ribak (February) are perhaps the biggest fine-art "names" of the project. Lozowick was probably alone in submitting for the calendar an image he had previously issued as a limited-edition stone lithograph: "Strike Scene," printed in 1934 in an edition of 10.[6] For the calendar Lozowick's 1934 print was photographically reproduced, with a slightly altered signature; all of the other sheets of the calendar are, apparently, photo-offset reproductions of original drawings.

Phil Bard (May), Eitaro Ishigako (August), Russell T. Limbach (April), A. Redfield (July), Theodore Scheel (March), and Sol Wilson (October) were regular contributors of illustrations to leftist publications; works by all of them frequented the pages of, for example, *New Masses.* Of M. Pass (September), I have been able to find no other trace, and the unsigned January illustration, though archetypically thirties in style, may be only tentatively identified as by Jacob "Jack" Burke.[7]

Taken together, these illustrations represent the high seriousness of the graphic arts during the Great Depression and the approach to World War II. Can you imagine the little tykes in the Upper West Side flat flipping over the pages of this calendar? No Easter bunnies for April; instead, barbed wire, a huge skull, and fascist salutes. Yes, there's an angel for December—but not a very Christmas-like one, not with its wings of swords and swastikas. Gloom, doom, and destruction are just about everywhere.

At the same time, these illustrations make untenable the charge frequently leveled at thirties art: that it, at least after the Soviets under Stalin installed Social Realism as official doctrine, was unredeemably awful and monolithic. Richard Fitzgerald, in a sympathetic but bittersweet account of *New Masses,* vividly expresses this disparaging view:

Socialist realism appeared to be a less distorted view of reality simply because it was, stylistically, a more conventional and academic view. Indeed, it employed some of the stylistic devices of the worst

3.3 Eitaro Ishigaki, illustration for American League Against War and Fascism calendar, 1936, one page of twelve.

bourgeois calendar art. Thus, most *New Masses* artists were caught in the aesthetic trap of their own debilitating and inadequate theories about art.[8]

But is this true? In the 1936 calendar, really only Bard, Ishigaki, Lozowick, Wilson, and the artist of January work in a manner that can be identified with Social Realism. Dehn, Gropper, Limbach, and (especially) Ribak are much too expressionistic. Pass is almost a Surrealist. Scheel comes out of Aubry Beardsley. And Redfield's bathing plutocrats, absent the magazine and given a proper punchline, could grace the pages of many an upscale publication (the *New Yorker* or *Esquire,* for example).

Yes, during the 1930s the once near-total iden-

tification of constructivist design and typography with the political Left came unraveled. And yes, again, many graphic artists who worked for publications on the Left adopted or adapted a version of Social Realism. But as this calendar of the American League Against War and Fascism demonstrates, thirties political art could and did come in a wide spectrum of styles.

NOTES

1. From a paper on graphic art delivered at the First American Artists' Congress in 1936 and reprinted in Matthew Baigell and Julia Williams, eds., *Artists against War and Fascism* (New Brunswick, New Jersey: Rutgers University Press, 1986), 137.

2. From a paper on the magazine and the artist delivered at the First American Artists' Congress in 1936 and reprinted in Baigell and Williams, *Artists against War,* 135.

3. From an introduction to the exhibition catalog, *America Today: A Book of 100 Prints* (first published in New York in 1936 by the American Artists' Congress; reissued as *Graphic Works of the American Thirties,* Da Capo Press, New York, 1977), 10.

4. Ibid., p. 7.

5. The copy of the calendar illustrated in this article was kindly put on extended loan to the University of New Mexico Art Museum by Beatrice Mandelman, herself a graphic artist during the 1930s, who then specialized in both serigraphs and color lithographs.

6. Janet Flint, *The Prints of Louis Lozowick: A Catalogue Raisonné* (New York: Hudson Hills Press, 1982), 113, no. 121.

7. Burke, onetime editorial cartoonist for the St. Louis *Post-Dispatch,* was a friend of Louis Ribak and Beatrice Mandelman and a frequent contributer to leftist publications and projects.

8. Richard Fitzgerald, *"New Masses,"* in *The American Radical Press,* ed. by Joseph R. Conlin (Westport, Conn.: Greenwood Press, 1974), vol. 2, 544.

HARRY GOTTLIEB

Artist, Printmaker, Political Activist,
Gentle Radical, Friend

Ellen Sragow

Hughie Lee-Smith's tribute to Harry Gottlieb,
who died at ninety-eight on July 4, 1992, beautifully summarizes the beliefs by which Harry lived.

> I remember Harry Gottlieb, first and foremost, as a
> wonderful human being; one who was always there
> with a helping hand and a word of encouragement.
> He was a man of principle who would brook no com-
> promise and, as a man of the people, his art gave
> expression to the needs and aspirations of those who
> could not speak for themselves.[1]

Harry Gottlieb was an artist whose work encompassed the social and political issues that
"consumed" him throughout his life. He depicted
people at work; the employed and the unem-
ployed; strikers and protesters; men, women, and
children of all races. For Harry art improved life.
His "job" was to make art accessible to the general public; accessible to the very people that he
portrayed in his work.

LITHOGRAPHY

Harry began his printmaking career during the
years he lived in Woodstock, New York (1923–
32).[2] When he received a Guggenheim Fellowship
to go to Europe, in 1931–32, he was already well-
prepared. He went to Paris and created a series of
black-and-white lithographs with the well-known
printer Edmond Desjobert. According to Harry,
these prints were

> . . . the best lithographs I ever made. I was very
> fortunate. Paris had the best lithographer probably
> in the world . . . Desjobert. He was a wonderful,
> wonderful lithographer.[3]

Desjobert was willing to experiment with the
stone, allowing Harry to push the technique further than he had done during his printmaking
days in Woodstock.

> There was an attractive, silky richness to Des-
> jobert's printing, which reflected in part his style
> as a printer, in part the character of the French inks
> with which he printed and in part his use of chine
> collé: a technique which makes possible the greatest
> of subtleties.[4]

One of the prints Harry produced there was *Unloading at Majorca* (figure 4.1). The print, created
with liquid tusche, had the appearance of a wash

drawing. This was one of Harry's early depictions
of men at work, a theme he would pursue more
actively during his years on the WPA.

Upon completion of his Guggenheim Fellowship, Harry returned to Woodstock. This was
the Depression, and there was talk among artists
of trying to get some financial support. Juliana
Force, director of the Whitney Museum, who had
given Harry his first one-man show in 1929, was
already working to raise funds and had the support of the artists. Gottlieb worked toward this
cause. Eventually all of the artists' efforts, as well
as the efforts of other groups and individuals, led
to the formation of the PWAP (Public Works of
Art Project) in December 1933.

In 1935 Harry became involved with the WPA,
and in 1936 he was assigned to the Graphics Division. There he created the black-and-white lithograph *Coal Pickers* (figure 4.2), which depicts a
group of people working the coalfields of a mining area. The central figures are women, bending
over to gather the coal. This was an unusual scene,
since most of the coal-mining prints created during that period by other artists depicted women as
miners' wives, not as workers.

Harry's first studio in New York was on Fifth
Avenue and Fourteenth Street. From his window
he would observe a beauticians' school, and he
made a series of drawings that led to the final version of the WPA lithograph *Beauticians Academy*

(figure 4.3). The impact of this image is strengthened through Gottlieb's use of a perspective that emphasizes a row of hanging lamps, receding into the distance.

In 1937 the Graphic Arts Division of the WPA was instrumental in revitalizing color lithography as a fine-art medium. At the time it was only being used for commercial purposes. Harry created several color lithographs, including *Bootleg Mining* (figure 4.4). In this five-color print he made use of tusche, crayon, and wash.

This powerful mining scene depicts a group of Pennsylvania coal miners working illegally at a closed mine in order to earn a meager living. The miners had to rig equipment up to the wheel rim of a truck or an automobile and use that vehicle's engine for power to help pull the coal up from the shaft. Harry had been required to become a member of the coal-miners' union in order to gain access to the mines so that he could accurately report on the situation. The role of the artist had become that of a reporter, and through his or her

4.3 Harry Gottlieb, *Beauticians Academy,* ca. 1936. WPA lithograph.

4.2 Harry Gottlieb, *Coal Pickers,* 1935–36. Lithograph.

4.4 Harry Gottlieb, *Bootleg Mining,* 1937. Color lithograph.

art, the artist could depict important events that might not have reached the public through any other medium.

Harry left the WPA in 1940, and by 1941 its artists were steadily turning their concerns toward the war. In 1941 Harry made the lithograph *Liberty* (figure 4.5). It depicts the United States and Miss Liberty welcoming the refugees escaping from the ravages of the war in Europe.

THE SILKSCREEN PROCESS

During his time with the WPA, in 1938, Harry was one of six artists (along with Ruth Chaney, Louis Lozowick, Eugene Morely, Hyman War-sager, and Elizabeth Olds) invited by Anthony Velonis to form a group to experiment with silkscreen as a fine-art medium. Up until that time, it had been used only for commercial purposes and for printing posters for the Poster Division of the WPA. Harry liked lithography but felt that the silkscreen was a more immediate process. "Lithography is a great process but you can't carry a lithographic stone around."[5]

The silkscreen process allowed the artist to be more independent. It did not require a specific workshop and heavy, expensive machinery. Artists could live anywhere; they could take their workshops with them. Because silkscreen was such a portable medium, Harry was able to travel around the country to colleges and universities,

4.5 Harry Gottlieb, *Liberty,* 1941. WPA lithograph.

demonstrating the process and allowing students to experiment. Other benefits of the process were that less-expensive paper could be used and larger editions could be produced, allowing prints to be sold for from $5 to $10 apiece; this expanded the buying audience. Harry felt that this "democratized" art, which was then accessible to the general public, rather than only to an elite group of collectors and museums.

The WPA did adopt the Silk Screen Unit into the Graphic Arts Division, and Harry did very innovative work. Silkscreen was a versatile medium, allowing the artist to use the ink in a variety of ways: thick and opaque, like oil paint; or thinner and more transparent, like watercolor.

The first truly major exhibition of silkscreen prints was Harry Gottlieb's solo show at the ACA Gallery in New York in March 1940. Its director, Henry Baron, was interested in and supportive of the ideas of a group of artists referred to as Social Realists. He was impressed with Gottlieb's skills. The show had much critical success and was important, since it publicized a distinctly American contribution to the graphic arts. One of the most important silkscreens Harry created was the ten-color print *The Strike is Won* (figure 4.6). Here he depicted a group of workers of many races celebrating a successful labor strike.

Gottlieb's imagery and style had an immediate impact. In his work there is usually a figure or group of figures in the foreground. The scenes are filled with movement and excitement. Flames and smoke arise from a foundry or mill. People raise their arms in protest or praise. Gottlieb was able to get viewers involved with the action of the scene almost as if they were participants in the event. Gottlieb's use of strong color and repetition of pattern added to the drama of the work. Since his style combined flat planes and areas of color with some contour, rather than explicit detail, Harry referred to it as "Social Content," rather than "Social Realism."

ART AND POLITICS

Gottlieb's political and social imagery of the 1930s and early 1940s was as powerful as the work done by the artists who had influenced him: the Mexican muralists Rivera, Siqueiros, Orozco, and the artists of the Russian Avant-Garde, who were working up until 1932. These artists connected themselves with political revolution through their art. During the cultural revolution in Russia, the People's Commission for Development and the Ministry of Culture were able to bring about certain changes. They were able to reorganize art education, museums, and the distribution of art. For a brief period the Avant-Garde changed from an underground movement to one whose artistic leadership influenced many institutions. Harry was able to accomplish similar goals in the United States, through his participation in the Artists' Union, the American Artists' Congress, and the American Artists' School. He became deeply involved with any project he worked on or any organization he worked with. Gottlieb's commitment was total.

Harry was one of the organizers of the Artists' Union, formed out of a group known as the UAG, United Artists' Group, and he went on to become its president in 1936. It was a division of the CIO.[6] The artists identified with the labor movement, since they were employees of the United States government under the Federal Arts Programs. The union fought for the rights of all workers, in order to improve economic and social conditions in the country. According to Lou Barlow,

> The Grievance Committee of the Artists Union intervened for artists who had problems with the administration. . . . There were arbitrary dismissals of non-citizens. Artists were required to sign in at a central station at 9 A.M. each morning to remain in his or her studio all day in the event there was an unannounced spot-check from a time-keeper. If there was no answer to a knock on the door, the artist would lose a week's salary. Under pressure from the Union, these indignities were eventually discontinued.[7]

Harry was a member of the American Artists' Congress and sat on its National Executive Committee. He was one of the artists who organized the first meeting in May 1935, set up to form the congress. On February 14, 15, and 16, 1936, the congress held its first meetings in New York City, at Town Hall and at the New School for Social Research. The 360 members from the United States and Mexico (including Orozco and Siqueiros) voted to form a permanent organization headed by Stuart Davis. The congress could speak for the unity of artists with regard to their economic and cultural security and freedom. The organization fought against war and Fascism, the destroyers of art and culture.

Harry read a paper at the Second Closed Session of the congress on the topic of "Problems of the American Artist." He chose to speak on the "Municipal Art Center." Gottlieb proposed that municipal art centers be formed, since he felt that art dealers and museums were not giving enough tangible support to living artists. They needed more visibility, and the centers would stimulate public interest and sales through exhibitions. Artists would make sure that there would be no censorship of works submitted for exhibition and no exclusion of noncitizens by the administration.

Censorship and discrimination were both issues addressed by the artists upon hearing Mayor La Guardia's proposal for a Municipal Art Center to be opened in early 1936 at 62 West Fifty-third Street. La Guardia gave his hand-picked "Committee of 100" the authority to determine which artists could exhibit (they had to be United States

citizens) and which works could be displayed. The artists protested and the policies were revised.

Harry urged his fellow artists throughout the country to set up municipal art centers and suggested that they be expanded to include art-rental libraries, with rental fees going to the artists, and art schools.

The American Artists' School on West Fourteenth Street in New York City, an outgrowth of the John Reed Club, was founded by Harry along with Stuart Davis, William Gropper, and Paul Manship. The John Reed School of Art emphasized political and social imagery that was in harmony with the working class. The American Artists' School expanded upon that ideal to include those artists whose imagery was abstract and whose interests covered a broader base of American culture. It was set up by the Artists' Union to assist and encourage minorities in gaining access to the WPA. Artists volunteered their time to

teach at the American Artists' School and many, including Yasuo Kuniyoshi and Anton Refregier, made lithographs to raise funds for the institution. This was part of a campaign to create dignity and equality for all artists.

Harry was always fighting for a cause, and he had been a great supporter of a federal art bill, which would have set up permanent funding for the arts—a permanent arts project. The bill had proposed a Department of Science, Art, and Literature. Unfortunately it was defeated.

Harry Gottlieb remained politically active well into his eighties. If there was a march being organized, he would be there. If there was a table being set up for leafletting, he would be there. If a meeting needed to be organized, his home was always available. He fought for human rights and freedom of expression. He believed that one must always continue the fight and never take freedom for granted, since it can be taken away so easily

4.7 Portrait of Harry Gottlieb at age 93, 1987.

through government repression, censorship, racism, and the breakdown of human values.

In 1970 Harry designed a card to raise funds for the Angela Davis Legal Defense Fund. He depicted the Statue of Liberty as an African-American woman. On the card Harry chose to include a quote from a Pablo Neruda poem, "Let the Rail Splitter Awake,"

> . . . let them march, singing and smiling,
> The young white, the young black
> Against the walls of gold,
> Against the manufacturer of hate,
> Against the merchant of their blood,
> Let them sing, laugh and conquer.[8]

Harry Sternberg speaks for all who knew and loved Harry Gottlieb:

> Harry Gottlieb and I shared many years of meetings, demonstrations, and art exhibitions out of which grew a warm and loving friendship. I shall miss this generous gentle man.[9]

NOTES

1. Statement received from Hughie Lee-Smith, September 1992.

2. There were several artists who printed in Woodstock during those years. Bolton Brown went there to set up a press in 1916 and printed for others from 1919 until around 1925. In 1929 the Woodstock Artists Association had acquired a lithography press. Grant Arnold came to Woodstock to print in 1930. There he was appointed printer for the WPA. He printed for Woodstock artists from 1930 until 1939. Emil Ganso printed lithographs there until 1939.

3. Sheryl Conkelton and Gregory Gilbert, *Harry Gottlieb, The Silkscreen and Social Concern in the WPA Era,* (Rutgers: State University of New Jersey), 22.

4. Clinton Adams, *American Lithographers 1900–1960: The Artists and Their Printers* (Albuquerque: University of New Mexico Press), 74.

5. Stephen Neil Greengard, ed., "Ten Crucial Years. The development of the United States Government Sponsored Artists Programs 1933–1943. A Panel Discussion by Six WPA Artists." *Journal of Decorative and Propaganda Arts (DAPA)* (Spring 1986): 55. The panel was organized by Ellen Sragow and moderated by Mitchell Wolfson, Jr. It was held March 30, 1985, at Miami Dade Community College and sponsored by the Mitchell Wolfson, Jr., Collection of Decorative and Propaganda Arts.

6. "UAA Local 60 UOPWA-CIO" was often printed on works of the period. The initials refer to United American Artists, Local 60, United Office and Professional Workers of America, Committee of Industrial Organizations.

7. Lou Barlow, "A Short History of the WPA/FAP with Emphasis on the Artists' Union," unpublished ms., 4.

8. Card distributed by the Open Gate Committee (New York City) for the Angela Davis Legal Defense Fund, 1970.

9. Statement received from Harry Sternberg, October 1992.

And *American Prize Prints of the 20th Century* in 1949 featured seven prints with black subjects; only one of the artists was African-American.[24] The proliferation of images of African-Americans in the prints of white artists of this period has not yet been fully explored, although some of the artists' interest can be attributed to the desire to portray American images,[25] and some as protest against the plight of the African-American.[26]

Gwathmey turned away from the rural South in *Watching Parade* or *Parade* (9); the image of a well-dressed urban white man, in a luxurious interior setting, is exceptional in Gwathmey's prints. Rosalie Gwathmey describes the figure as a "fat, gross Capitalist, standing not too near the balcony, staring down contemptuously at the people below."[27] Gwathmey, involved with left-ist politics from the thirties onward, conveys his message subtly in *Parade;* without Rosalie Gwathmey's interpretation, it could be misread. Indeed, as Lerner points out, Gwathmey's works are rarely overtly critical or accusing.[28] But *Non-Fiction* (5) is ferocious; as Brown says, "Who can forget in *Non-Fiction* the juxtaposition of the little black girl holding a child in her arms, surrounded by barbed wire, against the painted stereotype of a headless cutout mannequin minstrel playing a banjo?"[29]

In *Farmer's Wife* (12) Gwathmey introduces a new image into his prints, an elderly African-American women; she is seated, and uncharacteristically for Gwathmey's oeuvre, her hands lie idle in her lap. Gwathmey spoke of her more than once: "*Farmer's Wife* is my response to a lady of character who has borne the scars of outrageous circumstance and has refused to be destroyed."[30] And, "I know this farmer's wife; I know her husband, her children and her children's children. I know the relatives who have moved to the city. Also, I know the people for whom she works. . . . It was my hope that . . . I might have been able to extend the dignity and beauty of this lady. . . ."[31]

The figure, or a similar one, appears in *Matriarch* (16); these women and *Vendor* (19) all wear patterned dresses, a reminder that Rosalie Gwathmey was a textile designer, but also inaugurating a change in style. Gwathmey's style gradually became more decorative, with the areas of color set off by black lines, producing a stained-glass effect; the influence of stained glass was noted by his friend the artist Raphael Soyer (1899–1987) and confirmed by Gwathmey, who wrote from Paris to a friend in New York in 1949: "After visiting the Cathedral at Chartres, I was willing to believe that the stained glass there was the finest visual art expression ever. I still think it can't be beat."[32] The new style also appears in *Ring-Around-A-Rosy* (10) and is fully developed in *Vendor* (19) and *Flower Vendor* (20).

In the early sixties, Gwathmey made his only woodblock print (15) and his first lithograph, a self-portrait, with Burr Miller (13). Of the lithograph he said, "Now from my point of view it's not a lithograph. It is just a drawing in a grease crayon on a stone, without any exploration of the true media."[33] He continued to make lithographs for the next twenty years, frequently by request, for a gallery opening or for the benefit of a charity, but they were always "drawings in a grease crayon on stone." He taught drawing at Cooper Union and was thoroughly comfortable with the grease pencil, if not with lithography.

Because Gwathmey's color is so emphatic, it is possible to overlook the quality of his drawing. Yet according to Milton Brown,

> . . . the structure of Gwathmey's style lies in the drawing. One should study Gwathmey's drawings without the intrusion of color . . . to appreciate the uniqueness and quality of his line—taut, wiry, rhythmic, subtly balanced and melodically elegant, a line that does not so much define form as exist as an expressive element in itself. . . . All the bent weariness of the toiling sharecropper, an echo of Millet's heroic peasant without romanticism, is diagrammed in Gwathmey's incisive line. And his work is full of such haunting images of ricketic bodies, sagging shoulders, gnarled hands, and tragic faces, as well as moments of ineffable beauty and pathos.[34]

In the mid-sixties, when he was nearly seventy, Gwathmey moved to Long Island and rarely thereafter visited the South. His subject matter changed; he said he was "acutely aware of his immediate surroundings," and he became interested in flowers, especially wildflowers. And he added,

"Living on Long Island now there is the itinerant vegetable picker and fruit picker who is the man I knew in Virginia and North Carolina."[35] While his new imagery no longer centered on the South or the African-American, he sometimes revived old motifs, as in *Hoeing* (21).

The images in Gwathmey's late prints, *Tin of Lard* (18), *Migrant* (24), *Stargazing* (23), *Vendor* (19), *Petrouchka* (25), and so on, seem to belong to no particular time or place, although perhaps, as he suggested, they were inspired by what he saw around him. Robert Gwathmey died in 1988, and he was ill for several years before he died. But he continued to give interviews, and in one of them he said, "I've never compromised. Come hell or high water, I have painted what I want to paint."[36]

His last print, made as a contribution to Southampton Hospital, portrays a familiar figure in overalls, engaged in a routine task. The print is a reminder of a statement he made twenty years earlier: "I like medieval sculpture because those figures are not too unlike, say, Share Croppers. Share Croppers are thin and wiry and rheumatic. . . . In doing Share Croppers you'll find that there's never any elaborated action."[37]

Of the many critics and historians who have commented on Gwathmey's art, John Canaday's summation is most apt:

> Robert Gwathmey has been exceptional among the small minority of artists who can be called social

commentators. He has managed to capitalize on the sheer pictorial interest of his subject matter without reducing it to picturesqueness; he has recognized the poignance of the lives he paints without sentimentalizing them, and he has spoken of social injustice without mounting the soapbox.[38]

NOTES

1. I wish to express my thanks to Professor Diane Kelder of the Art History Department of the Graduate School and University Center of the City University of New York, under whose supervision this project began. I also wish to thank Philip Alexander, Will Barnett, Sylvan Cole, Terry Dintenfass, Rosalie Gwathmey, Jean Hoffmann, David Kiehl, Linda Kramer, Shelley Langdale, Jack Levine, Burr Miller, Mary Ryan, Harry Sternberg, Dan Weldon, and Dave Williams for their assistance.

2. Elizabeth McCausland, "Robert Gwathmey," *Magazine of Art,* April 1946, 149.

3. Ibid., 149.

4. Robert Gwathmey, unpublished interview with Arlene Jacobowitz, Brooklyn (Brooklyn Museum, September 29, 1966), n.p.

5. Charles K. Piehl, "A Southern Artist at Home in the North," *The Southern Quarterly* 26(1)(Fall 1987):6.

6. Telephone interview with Harry Sternberg, April 5, 1986.

7. Harry Salpeter, "Gwathmey's Editorial Art," *Esquire* (June 1944):131.

8. Telephone interview with Will Barnet, February 28, 1992.

9. See Reba and Dave Williams, *The Mexican Muralists and Prints,* exhibition catalogue (New York: 1990), for the mural influence on prints.

10. Robert Gwathmey, comment, in Albert Reese, *American Prize Prints of the 20th Century* (New York: American Artists Group, 1949), 73.

11. Charles K. Piehl, "The Eutaw Mural and the Southern Art of Robert Gwathmey," *The Alabama Review* 45(2)(April 1992):119.

12. Ellen G. Landau, *Artists for Victory,* exhibition catalogue (Washington, D.C.: Library of Congress, 1983), 2–3 and 44–45.

13. Jonathan Ingersoll, *Robert Gwathmey,* exhibition catalogue (St. Mary's City, Md.: St. Mary's College of Maryland, 1976), 8.

14. Robert Gwathmey, "Reminiscence," Studs Terkel, ed., *Hard Times* (New York: Pantheon, 1986), 374.

15. Robert Gwathmey, "Serigraphy," *American Artist* (December 1945):8.

16. Piehl, "A Southern Artist," 6.

17. Robert Gwathmey interviewed by Paul Cummings, March 5, 1968, typescript (New York: Archives of American Art), 32.

18. Interview with Harry Sternberg, August 24, 1991. In his interview with Paul Cummings, Gwathmey several times mentioned that he painted slowly.

19. Cummings interview, p. 32.

20. Gwathmey, "Serigraphy," 8; and Abram Lerner, "Robert Gwathmey Observed," in Helen A. Harrison, *Gwathmey Works from 1941–1983,* exhibition catalogue (East Hampton: Guild Hall, 1984), 7, says he is "closer to the aesthetics of Charles Sheeler and Fernand Léger than to those for whom it used to be said 'art is a weapon.'"

21. Milton W. Brown, *Robert Gwathney Drawings, Watercolors, and Paintings* (New York: Houghton Gallery, Cooper Union, 1985), n.p.

22. McCausland, "Robert Gwathmey," 149–50.

23. Landau, *Artists for Victory,* 13, 17, 35, 52, 83, 96, 120. Artists' interest in African-American participation in the war, especially in the African-American as defense worker, was probably inspired by the integration of the defense industry in 1941, by executive order of President Roosevelt, following the threat of an African-American protest march on Washington. The armed forces remained segregated until 1948; Jervis Anderson, *This Was Harlem 1900–1950* (New York: Noonday Press, 1981), 291–92.

24. Albert Reese, *American Prize Prints of the 20th Century* (New York: American Artists Group, 1949), 23, 60, 62, 69, 94, 140, 212. The artists are Julius Bloch, Isaac Friedlander, Michael J. Gallagher, Marion Greenwood, Edgar Imler, Blanche McVeigh, and John Wilson, who was the sole African-American.

25. In the thirties and forties, American artists sought to assert local American style and subjects; the image of the African-American had been used since at least the mid-nineteenth century to establish the "particularly American characteristics of a scene." Guy C. McElroy, *Facing History, The Black Image in American Art 1710–1940* (Washington, D.C.: The Corcoran Gallery, 1990), xiii.

26. In the late twenties, race relations in the United States seemed to improve, but in the 1930s the lynching rate began to rise, and artists focused on the issue; in 1935 more than three dozen artists participated in the exhibition "An Art Commentary on Lynching." See David Levering Lewis, *When Harlem was in Vogue* (New York: Oxford University Press), 215, 284; and M. Sue Kendall, *Rethinking Regionalism: John Steuart Curry and the Kansas Mural Controversy* (Washington, D.C.: Smithsonian, 1986), 78–80, 148–49, n. 69.

27. Telephone interview with Rosalie Gwathmey, September 12, 1992.

28. Lerner, "Robert Gwathmey," 7.

29. Milton W. Brown, *Robert Gwathmey Drawings, Watercolors and Paintings.*

30. Robert Gwathmey, "Statement by the Artist, 1972," in Abram Lerner, ed. *The Hirshhorn Museum and Sculpture Garden* (New York: 1974), 699.

31. Robert Gwathmey, (Statement), in *Contemporary Painting and Sculpture* (Urbana, Illinois: University of Illinois, 1953), 186.

32. Judd Tully, "Robert Gwathmey," *American Artist* (June 1985):90.

33. Cummings interview, 32.

34. Brown, *Robert Gwathmey,* n.p.

35. Cummings interview, 14.

36. Barbara Delatiner, "He Paints What Is in His Heart," *New York Times,* July 22, 1984, section 11, p. 13.

37. Cummings interview, 16.

38. John Canaday, in Ingersoll, *Robert Gwathmey,* n.p.

A BIBLIOGRAPHY

ACA Gallery. *Robert Gwathmey.* Exhibition catalogue. New York, January–February, 1946.

——— . *Outstanding Prints by American Artists.* New York, n.d.

Ackley, Clifford S., and Shelly R. Langdale. *American Screenprints: 1930s–1960s.* Exhibition checklist. Boston: Museum of Fine Arts, 1991.

Acton, David. *A Spectrum of Innovation: Color in American Printmaking 1890–1960.* Exhibition catalogue. Worcester, Mass.: Worcester Art Museum, 1990 (pp. 164–65).

Anderson, Jervis. *This Was Harlem 1900–1950.* New York: Noonday Press, 1981.

Beall, Karen F. *American Prints in the Library of Congress: A Catalog of the Collection.* Baltimore: Johns Hopkins Press, 1970 (p. 184).

Brown, Milton W. "Robert Gwathmey." In Marilyn Hoffner, *Robert Gwathmey: Drawings, Watercolors and Paintings.* Exhibition catalogue. New York: Houghton Gallery, The Cooper Union, 1985.

Bundy, David S. *Painting in the South: 1564–1980.* Exhibition catalogue. Richmond, Va.: Virginia Museum, 1983 (pp. 128–30, 136, 303).

Christie's. *Important American Paintings, Drawings and Sculpture of the 18th, 19th and 20th Centuries* catalogue. New York: December 6, 1991.

Clark-Langager, Sarah. *Order and Enigma: American Art Between the Two Wars.* Exhibition catalogue. Utica, N.Y.: Museum of Art, Munson-Williams-Procter Institute, 1984 (pp. 48–49).

Cole, Sylvan. *The Graphic Work of Joseph Hirsch.* New York: Associated American Artists, 1970.

Colt, Thomas C. *Robert Gwathmey.* Richmond, Va.: Museum of Fine Arts, Virginia Artists Series, No. 28, n.d.

Delatiner, Barbara. "He Paints What Is in His Heart." *New York Times,* July 22, 1984, section 11, p. 13.

William Doyle Galleries. *Old Master and Modern Prints Catalogue.* New York: December 15, 1989, p. 18.

Gwathmey, Robert. Interview by Paul Cummings. Typescript. New York: Archives of American Art, 1968.

——— . Interview by Arlene Jacobowitz. Brooklyn: The Brooklyn Museum, 1966.

——— . "Reminiscence." In *Hard Times,* ed. by Studs Terkel. New York: Pantheon, 1986 (pp. 373–76).

——— . "Serigraphs." *American Artist* (December 1945):8–11.

——— . "Statement by the Artist, 1972." In Abram Lerner, *The Hirshhorn Museum and Sculpture Garden.* New York: 1974 (p. 699).

——— . "Statement." In *Contemporary Painting and Sculpture.* Urbana, Ill.: University of Illinois, 1953 (p. 186).

Harrison, Helen A. *Gwathmey Works from 1914–1983.* Exhibition catalogue. East Hampton, N.Y.: Guild Hall Museum, 1984.

Hoffner, Marilyn. *Robert Gwathmey: Drawings, Watercolors and Paintings.* Exhibition catalogue. New York: Houghton Gallery, The Cooper Union, 1985.

Ingersoll, Jonathan. *Robert Gwathmey.* Exhibition catalogue. St. Mary's City, Md.: St. Mary's College of Maryland, 1976.

Kendall, M. Sue. *Rethinking Regionalism: John Steuart Curry and the Kansas Mural Controversy.* Washington, D.C.: Smithsonian Institution, 1986 (pp. 78–80, 148–49 n. 69).

Landau, Ellen G. *Artists for Victory.* Exhibition catalogue. Washington, D.C.: Library of Congress, 1983.

Lewis, David Levering. *When Harlem Was in Vogue.* New York: Oxford University Press, pp. 215, 284).

McCausland, Elizabeth. "Robert Gwathmey." *Magazine of Art* (April 1946): 148–52.

McElroy, Guy C. *Facing History: The Black Image in American Art 1710–1940.* Exhibition catalogue. Washington, D.C.: The Corcoran Gallery, 1990 (p. xiii).

Piehl, Charles K. "Anonymous Heroines: Black Women as Heroic Types in Robert Gwathmey's Art." In *Heroines of Popular Culture,* ed. by Pat Browne. Bowling Green, Ohio: Bowling Green State University Popular Press, 1987 (pp. 128–48).

———. "The Eutaw Mural and the Southern Art of Robert Gwathmey." *Alabama Review* 45(2)(April 1992):103–31.

———. "A Southern Artist at Home in the North: Robert Gwathmey's Acceptance of His Identity." *Southern Quarterly* 26(1)(Fall 1987):1–17.

———. "The Southern Social Art of Robert Gwathmey." *Transactions of the Wisconsin Academy of Sciences, Arts and Letters* 73 (1985):54–62.

———. "Robert Gwathmey, The Social and Historical Context of a Southerner's Art in the Mid-Twentieth Century." *Arts in Virginia* 29(1)(1989):2–15.

Prescott, Kenneth W., and Emma-Stina Prescott. *The Complete Graphic Work of Jack Levine.* New York: Dover, 1984.

Rago, Louise Elliott. "Robert Gwathmey Speaks on the Artist." *School Arts* (59)(January 31, 1960):31–32.

Reese, Albert. *American Prize Prints of the 20th Century.* New York: American Artists Group, 1949 (p. 73).

Salpeter, Harry. "Gwathmey's Editorial Art." *Esquire* (June 1944):83, 131–32.

Schall, Ellen M., John Wilmerding, and David M. Sokol. *American Art: American Vision.* Exhibition catalogue. Lynchburg, Va.: Maier Museum of Art, Randolph-Macon Woman's College, 1990 (pp. 96–97).

Serigraph Quarterly 1(1)(February 1946)–5(3)(September 1950). See also, National Serigraph Society miscellaneous publications, such as *New Serigraphs by Members,* exhibition lists, etc.

Swann Galleries. *Works on Paper* catalogue. New York: June 15, 1989.

———. *Works on Paper* catalogue. New York: June 4, 1992.

Tully, Judd. "Robert Gwathmey." *American Artist* (June 1985):46–50, 88–91.

Williams, Reba, and Dave Williams. *American Screenprints from the Collection of Reba and Dave Williams.* Exhibition catalogue. New York: 1991.

———. "The Early History of the Screenprint." *Print Quarterly* III (December 1986):286–321.

———. *The Mexican Muralists and Prints.* Exhibition catalogue. New York: 1990.

AN ILLUSTRATED AND ANNOTATED CHECKLIST

1. *The Hitchhiker,* 1937.

RELATED PAINTING: *The Hitchhiker,* ca. 1936, Brooklyn
Museum.

MEDIUM: silkscreen

DIMENSIONS: Image: 16 13/16 × 13 1/8 in.;
42.7 × 33.3 cm.
Sheet: 23 9/16 × 17 1/16 in.; 59.9 × 43.3 cm.

PRINTER: unknown

PUBLISHER: unknown

EDITION: unknown; probably quite small.

COMMENT: The painting, 30 × 36, is one of Gwathmey's earliest surviving oil paintings; Gwathmey
destroyed most of his early work in 1938. Judd Tully,
a journalist who interviewed Gwathmey in 1985, says
the painting is autobiographical: "The shirt-sleeved
figure in the foreground, with thumb to the sky, could
well be the painter, heading back home to Richmond"
(48–49).

The print has been simplified and cropped, eliminating the telephone pole and several of the billboards.
Gwathmey has substituted a single, seated figure for
the two in the rear right of the painting. The print is
illustrated in Ackley and Langdale, *American Screenprints* (n.p.), and in Clark-Langager, *Order and Enigma*
(p. 49), among other places. Terry Dintenfass has seen
an impression dated in the artist's hand.

COLLECTIONS: Boston Museum of Fine Arts; British
Museum; Metropolitan Museum; Museum of Modern
Art; Munson-Williams-Proctor Institute; Reba and
Dave Williams.

2. *Rural Home Front,* 1943.

RELATED PAINTING: *The Farmer Wanted a Boy,* 1942,
loaned to ACA Gallery 1946 exhibition by Earle
Ludgin; not located.

MEDIUM: silkscreen

DIMENSIONS: Image: 10 1/4 × 18 1/4 in.;
26.0 × 46.4 cm.
Sheet: Various; largest is 16 × 22 3/4 in.; 40.6 × 57.8
cm.

PRINTER: unknown

PUBLISHER: unknown

EDITION: 100

COMMENT: The print received wide publicity for win-
ning the serigraph prize in the "America in the War"
contest (1943). It has been frequently reproduced,
both then and subsequently; for example, in Reese,
American Prize Prints (p. 73); Williams and Williams,
American Screenprints (p. 36); Piehl, "Eutaw Mural"
(p. 120); Swann, 1992 (#130). According to Landau
(*Artists for Victory,* pp. 2–3), the contest was announced
in May 1943, and works had to be submitted by August
1943. Editions were to be limited to 100. Gwathmey's
print was in the "Heroes of the Home Front" category.

The image in the print has been changed slightly
from that in the painting; the fieldworker in the upper
right hand corner of the painting has been replaced
with workers on their way to a factory. According
to Terry Dintenfass, the infant in both the painting
and the print is the artist's son, Charles Gwathmey (b
1939). An impression seen by Terry Dintenfass has an
alternate title, *Family Portrait,* verso.

COLLECTIONS: Butler Institute of American Art;
Library of Congress; MOMA; National Museum of
American Art; Reba and Dave Williams.

3. *Share Croppers*, 1944.

Alternate title, *Share Cropper*.

RELATED PAINTINGS: *Share Croppers*, 1939, was included and illustrated in the ACA Gallery 1946 catalogue; not located. An apparently identical painting, *Hoeing*, n.d., Rose Art Museum, Brandeis, is reproduced in Piehl, "Anonymous Heroines" (p. 132); the painting is still in the Rose Art Museum collection.

MEDIUM: silkscreen

DIMENSIONS: Image: 14½ × 12 in.; 36.8 × 30.5 cm. Sheet: 17 × 14* in.; 43.2 × 35.6* cm.

PRINTER: unknown

PUBLISHER: unknown

EDITION SIZE: unknown

COMMENT: The print is discussed and reproduced in Gwathmey, "Serigraphs" (p. 8). The print appeared in the fourth annual Exhibition of the National Serigraph Society, May 1944. The compositions of the print and the paintings appear to be identical. Beall, *American Prints*, reproduced it (p. 184), and dated it (1942). Terry Dintenfass has seen an impression entitled *Two Field Workers*, or *Hoeing*, verso, unknown hand. The Metropolitan Museum's impression is titled *Share Cropper*.

COLLECTIONS: Library of Congress; Metropolitan Museum.

* Possibly trimmed.

4. *End of Day*, 1944.

Alternate title, *Across the Field*, 1944.

RELATED PAINTINGS: *End of Day*, 1943, was illustrated in the ACA Gallery 1946 catalogue, loaned by I.B.M.; I.B.M. still owns the painting. *Serigraph Quarterly* 3(4)(November 1948) reports that a painting with this title was in the twenty-fourth Venice Biennale. A similar painting, with the title *Across the Fields*, nd, was reproduced in *Architectural Digest* (November 1983): 50 (not located).

MEDIUM: silkscreen

DIMENSIONS: Image: 12¼ × 14 in.; 31.1 × 35.6 cm. Sheet: 17 × 22 in.; 43.2 × 55.9 cm.

PRINTER: unknown

PUBLISHER: unknown

EDITION SIZE: unknown

COMMENT: The print is illustrated in Gwathmey, "Serigraphs" (p. 11), with the title *End of Day*. Gwathmey has slightly simplified the composition of the print, excluding two minor figures on the left that appear in the painting *End of Day*. The composition of the painting *Across the Fields* is somewhat different.

The print was included in the fourth annual exhibition of the National Serigraph Society, May 10–31, 1944, and was mentioned in *Serigraph Quarterly* 2 (May 1946) as chosen by the State Department as ideal decor for the modern home and used to decorate a prefabricated house in Brussels; also mentioned in *Serigraph Quarterly* 3(1)(February 1948) as being very popular in a recent USIS exhibition in Ceylon; mentioned in Members' Prints in Permanent Collections, October 29–December 1, 1945. But this print is not identified in those publications as having been published by the

National Serigraph Society. Terry Dintenfass has recorded an impression with the title *Across the Field,*
dated 1944, in the artist's hand.
COLLECTIONS: Mary Ryan Gallery.

5. *Non-Fiction,* (1945).

RELATED PAINTING: *Non-Fiction,* 1941, was illustrated
in the ACA Gallery 1946 catalogue, loaned by the
Encyclopaedia Brittanica. In 1951 the painting
was acquired from the Encyclopaedia Brittanica
by the University of Rochester Memorial Art Gal-
lery, where it remains. Rochester dates the painting
1943.
MEDIUM: silkscreen
DIMENSIONS: Image: $17\frac{1}{5} \times 13\frac{9}{10}$ in.;
43.7 × 35.3 cm.
Sheet: $21\frac{1}{2} \times 17$ in.; 54.7 × 43.3 cm.
PRINTER: unknown
PUBLISHER: unknown
EDITION SIZE: unknown
COMMENT: The print (not illustrated) is listed in
"Members' Prints in Permanent Collections," National
Serigraph Society, October 29–December 1, 1945.
An impression of the print sold at Swann Galleries,
June 15, 1989, and is illustrated in the catalogue, lot
107. The Swann description erroneously asserts that
"Gwathmey made only about 12 prints in his lifetime in
very small editions of 15–40 proofs."
COLLECTIONS: Metropolitan Museum.

6. *Singing and Mending*, 1946.

RELATED PAINTING: *Singing and Mending,* 1945, Hirshhorn Museum, was illustrated in the ACA Gallery 1946 catalogue. The Hirshhorn Museum still owns the painting. A spokesman for the Terry Dintenfass Gallery knows of a similar composition of 1941–42; not located.

MEDIUM: silkscreen

DIMENSIONS: Image: 12 × 14¼ in.; 30.7 × 36.3 cm. Sheet: 15¼ × 18⅔ in.; 38.8 × 47.4 cm.

PRINTER: unknown

PUBLISHER: National Serigraph Society

EDITION: 200

COMMENTS: The print is reproduced and discussed in Acton, *Spectrum,* (pp. 164–65). As Acton points out, the composition of the print has been simplified; for example, the pot on the table has been removed. The print is also cited in *Serigraph Quarterly* 1(3)(August 1946), "New Prints Published by the National Serigraph Society Since April 12, 1946."

Terry Dintenfass says this print was made in an unusual process. The prints were mounted on cardboard, and many people have thought they were paintings. Harry Sternberg believes that these early large-edition prints were printed by a professional printer; Rosalie Gwathmey concurs, adding that Gwathmey always used professional assistance in making prints.

COLLECTIONS: Art Institute of Chicago; Boston Museum of Fine Arts; Brooklyn Museum; Butler Institute of American Art; Fine Arts Museum of San Francisco; Worcester Museum.

7. *Topping Tobacco,* 1947.

RELATED PAINTING: *Topping Tobacco,* 1944, was illustrated in the 1946 ACA Gallery Exhibition; loaned by Mr. and Mrs. Milton Schwartz; not located.

MEDIUM: silkscreen

DIMENSIONS: Image: 13¼ × 8¾ in.; 33.7 × 22.2 cm. Sheet: 20 × 12¾ in.; 50.8 × 32.4 cm.

PRINTER: unknown

PUBLISHER: National Serigraph Society, "New Prints Published by the National Serigraph Society Since May 1, 1947."

EDITION: 300

COMMENT: Listed in *Serigraph Quarterly* 2(3)(August 1947); also illustrated in 8(2)(May 1948):2. Illustrated as well in Williams and Williams, "Early History" (p. 286). Terry Dintenfass owns an impression dated 1944 verso, entitled "Picking Tobacco." A Gwathmey print with the title *Topping Tobacco* sold at Swann Galleries, June 15, 1989, lot 109, not illustrated; the description inexplicably asserts that the impression sold was "one of 40."

COLLECTIONS: Butler Institute of American Art; Ed Ogul; Reba and Dave Williams.

8. *Tobacco Farmers,* 1947.

RELATED PAINTING: *Hoeing Tobacco,* 1946, Georgia
  Museum of Art, appears to be nearly identical in
  composition. In 1992 the Georgia Museum still
  owned the painting, which is illustrated in Bundy,
  Painting in the South (p. 303).

MEDIUM: silkscreen

DIMENSIONS: Image: 13 ½ × 10 ½ in.; 34.3 × 26.7 cm.
  Sheet: 16 × 13 ¼ in; 40.6 × 33.7 cm.

PRINTER: unknown

PUBLISHER: National Serigraph Society, "New Prints
  Published by the National Serigraph Society Since
  May 1, 1947."

EDITION: 300

COMMENT: Listed and illustrated in *Serigraph Quarterly,*
  3(3)(August 1947); edition and size information are
  from this source.

Collections: Butler Institute of American Art; Reba
and Dave Williams.

9. *Watching Parade* or *Parade,* (1947).

RELATED PAINTINGS: *Parade,* 1944, formerly in the
  Hirshhorn Museum's collection, sold at Christie's,
  December 6, 1991. Also, *Parade,* 1951, water-
  color, still in the Hirshhorn Museum collection. See
  Christie's, *Important American Paintings* (p. 199).

MEDIUM: silkscreen

DIMENSIONS: Image: 15 ⅜ × 11 ⅞ in.; 39.1 × 30.2 cm.
  Sheet: 22 ¼ × 17 ⅛ in.; 56.5 × 43.5 cm.

PRINTER: unknown

PUBLISHER: unknown

EDITION: unknown

COMMENT: Mentioned in *Serigraph Quarterly,* February 1948, as having been popular at a recent USIS
  exhibition in Ceylon. Reproduced in ACA Gallery one-
  page list of "Outstanding Prints by Famous American
  Artists," n.d., under the title *Watching Parade.*

COLLECTIONS: Butler Institute of American Art;
Metropolitan Museum; Reba and Dave Williams.

10. *Ring-Around-A-Rosy,* 1949.

RELATED PAINTING: *Children Dancing,* ca. 1948, at the Butler Institute of American Art, appears to be an identical composition; it is illustrated in Piehl, "Anonymous Heroines" (p. 145).

MEDIUM: silkscreen

DIMENSIONS: Image: 12⅝ × 15⅞ in.;
  32.1 × 40.3 cm.
  Sheet: 14¼ × 17½ in.; 36.2 × 44.5 cm.

PRINTER: unknown

PUBLISHER: National Serigraph Society, "New Prints Published Since February 1, 1949."

EDITION: 200

COMMENT: Cited and illustrated in National Serigraph Society, May 1949. An impression sold at Swann Galleries, June 4, 1992 (illustrated, #131), described as "Family Scene; Children Dancing." Terry Dintenfass has recorded an alternate title, *Ring Around Rosey.*

COLLECTIONS: Butler Institute of American Art; Reba and Dave Williams.

11. *Sowing* (ca. 1950)

RELATED PAINTING: *Sowing,* 1949, Whitney Museum of American Art, reproduced in Harrison, *Gwathmey Works* (p. 13), appears to be an identical composition.

MEDIUM: silkscreen

DIMENSIONS: Image: 16¼ × 17¼ in.;
  41.3 × 43.8 cm.
  Sheet: 17½ × 23 in.; 44.45 × 58.4 cm.

PRINTER: unknown

PUBLISHER: unknown

EDITION: unknown

COLLECTIONS: Private collection.

12. *Farmer's Wife,* 1954.

RELATED PAINTING: *Portrait of a Farmer's Wife,* 1951,
Hirshhorn Collection, reproduced in Ingersoll,
Robert Gwathmey; the catalogue entry dates the painting 1953. The 1951 date is the Hirshhorn's. *Field
Flowers,* 1946, Whitney Museum of American Art,
is a similar composition, reversed; and a photomechanical reproduction of this painting exists. A
related drawing, *Old Woman,* ca. 1946, is owned by
the Worcester Art Museum, reproduced in Acton,
Spectrum (p. 164).

MEDIUM: silkscreen

DIMENSIONS: Image: 17 × 13 ⅓ in.; 43.1 × 33.5 cm.
Sheet: 21 ½ × 15 ½ in.; 54.6 × 39.5 cm.

PRINTER: unknown

PUBLISHER: unknown

EDITION: 200

COMMENT: The Metropolitan Museum owns an impression of the print, dated 1954, edition 200. The
composition of the painting and the print appear to be
identical. The print sold at William Doyle Galleries,
December 15, 1989; it was illustrated in *Old Masters
and Modern Prints* catalog, page 18, titled *Grandmother.*
An impression sold at Swann Galleries, June 4, 1992;
it was illustrated in the catalogue (#129) and entitled
The Grandmother.

COLLECTIONS: Metropolitan Museum.

13. *Self-Portrait,* 1961.

RELATED PAINTINGS: This is the only self-portrait
Gwathmey ever made, but certain motifs from his
paintings appear in the print, such as the black crow,
which appears in *Standard Bearer,* 1946, Museu de
Arte Contemporânea da Universidade de São Paulo,
Brazil; and in *Poll Tax Country,* 1945, Hirschhorn
Museum and Sculpture Garden. Both are illustrated
in Piehl, "Robert Gwathmey" (pp. 4–5).

MEDIUM: lithograph

DIMENSIONS: Image: 17 ¼ × 15 in.; 43.8 × 38.1 cm.
Sheet: 26 ⅛ × 20 ⅛ in.; 66.4 × 51.1 cm.

PRINTER: George C. Miller and Son, Inc.

PUBLISHER: Terry Dintenfass, Inc.

EDITION: 50

COMMENTS: The print was made for the opening of
the Terry Dintenfass Gallery, New York City, when
Ms. Dintenfass asked each of the gallery artists to make
a lithograph self-portrait. The print is reproduced in
Piehl, "Southern Social Art" (p. 59).

COLLECTIONS: Flint Institute of Arts; Library of Congress; MOMA.

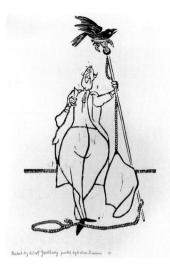

14. *A Section,* (1961).

RELATED DRAWING: *Section of Town,* 1969, reproduced
in Ingersoll, *Robert Gwathmey;* and in Hoffner, *Robert
Gwathmey.*

MEDIUM: lithograph

DIMENSIONS: Image: 13 ½ × 16 in.; 34.3 × 40.6 cm.
Sheet: 20 × 21 ¼ in.; 50.8 × 54.0 cm.

PRINTER: George C. Miller and Son, Inc.

PUBLISHER: Terry Dintenfass, Inc.

EDITION: 75

COMMENT: The print was included in the Heckscher
Museum 1972 exhibition but not reproduced in the
catalogue. Original lithograph for a Terry Dintenfass
Gallery opening.

COLLECTIONS: Private collection; Ed Ogul.

15. *The Senator,* 1962.

RELATED PAINTING: *Standard Bearer,* 1946, Museu de
Arte Contemporânea da Universidade de São Paulo,
Brazil, illustrated in Piehl, "Robert Gwathmey"
(p. 5).

RELATED DRAWING: *The Senator,* ca. 1932, reproduced
in Hoffner, *Robert Gwathmey* (n.p.); not located.

MEDIUM: woodblock

DIMENSIONS: Image: 18 × 11 in.; 45.7 × 27.9 cm.
Sheet: 20¾ × 14¾ in.; 52.7 × 37.5 cm.

PRINTER: Antonio Frasconi

PUBLISHER: none

EDITION: one impression only

COMMENT: A similar image, entitled *The Standard
Bearer,* was included in a portfolio of reproductive
prints published by the Graphic Workshop of New
York City in 1949, under the title "Negro: USA." *The
Standard Bearer* appears to be a mechanical reproduc-
tion of an ink drawing.

COLLECTIONS: The single impression, dated by Frasconi, is in a private collection.

16. *Matriarch,* 1962.

RELATED PAINTINGS: This print does not appear to
relate to a specific painting, but the figure is a type
portrayed in a number of Gwathmey's works.

MEDIUM: lithograph

DIMENSIONS: Image: 19 ½ × 15 ¼ in.; 49.5 × 38.7 cm.
Sheet: 26 × 20 in.; 66.0 × 50.8 cm.

PRINTER: George C. Miller and Son, Inc.

PUBLISHER: Terry Dintenfass, Inc.

EDITION: 50

COMMENT: The figure is related in type to that in print
11. See Piehl, "Anonymous Heroines," for a discussion
of African-American women in Gwathmey's paintings,
with several illustrations.

COLLECTIONS: Brooklyn Museum; Ed Ogul.

17. *Sharecropper,* (1969).

RELATED PAINTING: None identified. Despite the title,
the image is not related to print 3 or to its associated
paintings.

MEDIUM: lithograph

DIMENSIONS: Image: 14 ½ × 12 in.; 37.0 × 30.4 cm.
Sheet: 17 × 14 in.; 43.0 × 35.4 cm.

PRINTER: George C. Miller and Son, Inc.

PUBLISHER: Anti-Defamation League of B'nai Brith.

EDITION: 125

COMMENTS: One of seven lithographs in a portfolio, as
follows:

1. Arbit Blatas, *Babi Yar*
2. Robert Gwathmey, *Sharecropper*
3. Joseph Hirsch, *Cellist*
4. Jack Levine, *Cain and Abel*
5. Jacques Lipchitz, *Prometheus*
6. Abraham Rattner, *The Prophets*
7. Raphael Soyer, *Woman and Child*

Neither Gwathmey's print nor the portfolio is dated,
but the Levine print in the portfolio is dated 1969 in
Prescott and Prescott, *The Complete Graphic Work of Jack
Levine* (#52, p. xxv), and the Hirsch print is dated
1969 in Cole, *The Graphic Work of Joseph Hirsch* (#59,
n.p.).

COLLECTIONS: Brooklyn Museum.

18. *Tin of Lard* (1969).

RELATED DRAWING: A related drawing, ca. 1960 exists; not located.

MEDIUM: lithograph

DIMENSIONS: Image: 17½ × 13½ in.; 44.5 × 34.3 cm.
Sheet: 24 × 18 in.; 61.0 × 45.7 cm.

PRINTER: George C. Miller and Son, Inc.

PUBLISHER: Terry Dintenfass, Inc.

EDITION: 125

COMMENT: Reproduced in Heckscher Museum catalogue, 1972 (p. 8). A revised print was used in a poster for the School of Fine and Applied Arts Gallery, Boston University, February–March, 1969. See also print 26.

COLLECTIONS: Sylvan Cole.

19. *Vendor,* (1975).

RELATED PAINTING: *Vendor,* 1974, reproduced in Ingersoll, *Robert Gwathmey;* loaned to the exhibition by Dr. Louis Wener; not located. Also the vendor figure in the upper left of *Street Scene,* 1975, reproduced in the same catalogue.

MEDIUM: silkscreen

DIMENSIONS: Image: 36⅛ × 28⅛ in.;
91.8 × 71.4 cm.
Sheet: 40 × 32 in.; 101.6 × 81.3 cm.

PRINTER: Ives-Sillman

PUBLISHER: Terry Dintenfass, Inc.

EDITION: 125

COMMENT: The print sold at both Christie's and William Doyle Galleries in November and December 1991; it was reproduced in the Christie's catalogue (p. 36). The composition of the painting and the print appear to be identical.

COLLECTIONS: Private collection.

20. *Flower Vendor,* (ca. 1975).

RELATED PAINTING: *Flower Vendor,* date and location
   not known.

MEDIUM: silkscreen

DIMENSIONS: Image: 17 × 12 ¼ in.; 43.2 × 31.1 cm.
   Sheet: 23 ⅛ × 17 ½ in.; 58.7 × 44.5 cm.

PRINTER: unknown

PUBLISHER: unknown

EDITION: unknown

COLLECTIONS: Private collection.

21. *Hoeing,* (1978).

RELATED PAINTING: See paintings listed under print 3.

MEDIUM: lithograph

DIMENSIONS: Image: 24 ¼ × 18 ¼ in.;
   61.6 × 46.4 cm.
   Sheet: 29 ½ × 21 ¾ in.; 74.9 × 55.3 cm.

PRINTER: George C. Miller and Son, Inc.

PUBLISHER: Himan Brown

EDITION: 300

COMMENT: The composition of this print appears to be
identical to that of the serigraph *Share Croppers,* print 3.
This print, as well as prints 22 and 23, were published
as tax shelters.

COLLECTIONS: Ed Ogul

22. *Southern Farmer,* (1978).

RELATED DRAWING: *Man with Sack,* 1969, 29 × 22¾
in., not located.

MEDIUM: lithograph

DIMENSIONS: Image: 24¼ × 18¼ in.;
61.6 × 46.4 cm.
Sheet: 29½ × 21¾ in.; 74.9 × 55.3 cm.

PRINTER: George C. Miller and Son, Inc.

PUBLISHERS: Himan Brown

EDITION: 300

COMMENT: See print 21.

COLLECTIONS: Private collection.

23. *Stargazing,* (1978).

RELATED PENCIL DRAWING: *Stargazing,* 1974 (Terry
Dintenfass Gallery)

MEDIUM: lithograph

DIMENSIONS: Image: 24¼ × 18¼ in.;
61.6 × 46.4 cm.
Sheet: 29½ × 21¾ in.; 74.9 × 55.3 cm.

PRINTER: George C. Miller and Son, Inc.

PUBLISHER: Himan Brown

EDITION: 300

COMMENT: See print 21.

COLLECTIONS: Private collection.

24. *Migrant*, (1978).
Alternate title, *Tomato Picker.*
Related paintings: *Migrant,* 1976, illustrated in Ingersoll, *Robert Gwathmey*; in Harrison, *Gwathmey Works* (p. 14), from a private collection; not located.
MEDIUM: silkscreen
DIMENSIONS: Image: 27⅜ × 18¾ in.;
    69.5 × 47.6 cm.
    Sheet: 33 × 26 in.; 83.8 × 66.0 cm.
PRINTER: The Screenprint Workshop (Arnold Hoffman)
PUBLISHER: Five Towns Music and Art Foundation
EDITION: 200
COMMENT: Terry Dintenfass says this print was published by, and sold for the benefit of, Five Towns Music and Art Foundation.
COLLECTIONS: Private collection, Southampton Hospital.

25. *Petrouchka*, (1980).
Alternate title, *Ophelia.*
Related painting: *Petrouchka,* (1979), in the 1985 Cooper Union exhibition, illustrated in Hoffner, *Robert Gwathmey,* loaned by Terry Dintenfass Gallery; not located.
MEDIUM: silkscreen
DIMENSIONS: Image: 29½ × 22 in.; 74.9 × 55.9 cm.
    Sheet: 33 × 26 in.; 83.8 × 66.0 cm.
PRINTER: The Screenprint Workshop (Arnold Hoffmann)
PUBLISHER: Terry Dintenfass, Inc.
EDITION: 123 plus 30 artist's proofs
COLLECTIONS: Private collection.

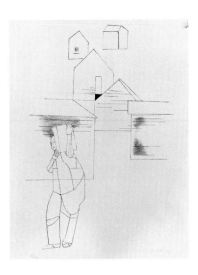

26. *(Mortar Carrier),* (1983).

RELATED DRAWING: see print 18.

MEDIUM: lithograph

DIMENSIONS: Image: 27 ½ × 22 ½ in.;
 69.9 × 57.2 cm.
 Sheet: 21 ½ × 15 in.; 54.6 × 38.1 cm.

PRINTER: Dan Weldon, Hampton Editions Ltd., Sag
 Harbor, New York.

PUBLISHER: Hampton Editions Ltd. and The Southampton Hospital.

EDITION: 100, plus not more than 20 artist's proofs.

COMMENT: According to Dan Weldon, (Mortar Carrier) is made from the same drawing that produced *Tin
of Lard,* reversed. It was produced for *The Southampton Hospital Portfolio, Works by 10 Major Artists of the
Hamptons.* The other artists were: Willem de Kooning,
Elaine de Kooning, James Brooks, Dan Flavin, Jimmy
Ernst, Robert Dash, Syd Solomon, Esteban Vicente,
and Paul Davis.

COLLECTIONS: Reba and Dave Williams

THE SKIN OF THE WORLD

Leon Golub and Nancy Spero

Lynne Allen

*They stand out vividly against a Pompeian red back-
ground, bold men, confrontational and seemingly 'in
control,' larger than life and frozen in time. Their ex-
pressions are brutal and raw, not unlike the surface of
the canvas they are painted on. The scene strikes a nerve
in each of us, and no matter how we deal with it—
denounce, ignore, or praise—no one walks away un-
touched. These instantaneous 'moments in time' belong to
the artist Leon Golub.*

*Hers, on the other hand, are delicate and fragile,
longitudinal 'journals' produced on thin skinlike paper,
seemingly ephemeral yet strong, like a woman. Hidden
among the luscious silvery whites on white are swastikas and tattoos, images of war and holocaust, images
of rebellion against victimization in feminist language.
Although the reaction is not immediate, these images
are equally arresting. They sneak up on you. The artist
who 'rolls and unrolls' her own skin through her work is
Nancy Spero.*

*Together they have managed to sustain a family and
maintain consistent but varied careers, producing images
that on the surface are poles apart yet are only 'skin'
(surface) deep. As I sat in their New York studio, removed from the violent sounds of the city, I felt curiously*

safe. The studio is just that—a large studio space divided down the middle—with very little 'living' space. Both Golub and Spero have studio assistants, young artists who receive good salaries and health benefits. The fact that their employees are protected, as they are protected, should not surprise anyone. Nor should anyone be surprised that they both did prints for the Democratic Party for women candidates. At the moment they have become, among other personae, social/political artists who deny inhumanity and whose work exposes the inadequacy of a miserable social reality.

One way to assess societies is to examine their histories and myths. For instance the myth of the American frontier was the 'Wild West,' the land of opportunity for those who went after it. Authority was challenged everywhere, and from this chaotic situation emerged a society very innovative, energetic, able to take risks, but also very violent. Today this same violence can be seen on our streets, in our homes, and in the world around us. Individually Leon Golub and Nancy Spero target many aspects of a diseased twentieth-century society, while searching for a fundamental 'self' or 'identity'— personal, cultural, social, sexual, and racial. For both, art is a means through which the "I" comes to grips with the world.

It has been stated that few Abstract Expressionist artists in America were interested in making prints during the late 1940s and early 1950s, and only began to make important contributions to the print medium during the print renaissance of the 1960s. Although we are led to believe that printmaking had nearly died out before 1960, there were active signs of a creative life in printmaking in many corners of the United States during this time. Leon Golub appropriated many of the improvisational techniques of Abstract Expressionist painting in his early (1946) 'primitive' print works, done first at the Southside Community Center in Chicago and later at The Art Institute of Chicago with Max Kahn in lithography and Vera Burdick in etching. The print workshop of Ellen Lanyon and Roland Ginzel also held an important place in his development. He remarks that "Ellen Lanyon and Roland Ginzel set up a print shop in the middle fifties in Chicago where they did litho and etching. They had studied with Lasansky and were very devoted. It was an open, welcoming workshop and held a very important place. Printmaking had not died out; that is a fable. What June Wayne subsequently brought back was printmaking in a public aspect."

Going down to the Southside Community Center, which was run by blacks in a black area before all the racial tension started, provided Golub with his initial introduction to prints.

My printmaking in the late forties was much rawer and maybe more original than my painting was. It was physically more intense as well as psychologically more intense. I found a process where I would work on something and wouldn't like the damn thing, and I would rework it and rework it. Originally it was a way of retrieving what was lost, but like erosion it showed the effects of what it had gone through. It was historical already, three days older! It took me to 1950 to do in painting what I had done in printmaking. I caught up with it. I developed a technique which I have been using ever since.

Golub's 'attack' on the litho stone was notorious at the Art Institute, where Spero also experimented with unique lithographs incorporating language. Eventually Golub was only allowed to work on the same few stones, often gouging them as deep as 1/16 of an inch. The rubbed and eroded surfaces of the prints led to experimentation with painting techniques that resulted in Golub's present style. He started in oils, which he gave up for porch paints, because oils were too 'buttery'; the porch paints were viscous and "nice and ugly." On unsized canvas they became part of the canvas, but on sized canvas they cracked, because the paints did not have plasticizers in them. This cracking became the beginning of a series of experiments using various tools to actually abrade the surface of the paint. He scraped them, but did not have an easy way to produce effects equivalent to that of the prints. Starting with dental tools, then sculpture tools, he finally succumbed to a

flat meat cleaver. Having built up layer upon layer of paint, he used solvents to soften and erode the paint, which he scraped off selectively. The final result is the characteristically brutal, veiled, and layered look of Golub's modern mercenaries. "I have been working this way ever since, but the initial significance of this technique came to me through the prints."

Golub's early work while at the Art Institute and later, after graduation, concentrated on a singular image that was totemic, highly stylized and condensed, very frontal, and influenced by primitive art of all kinds. Eventually, by the mid-fifties, Golub began to dislike what he was doing; he felt that he was churning around in his own subjectivity. It was too emotional and not leading anywhere. "I did a series of paintings called 'In Self' but I wanted to really go 'out-self.' There was an external world out there. The front plane of the painting is of course that point in time—what is there and what is here—sort of a skin, the skin of the world. You enter it, or pierce it, or it blocks you. How do you enter into space? Or how does space interpenetrate around you? So, I decided I wanted to articulate figures. I always could draw pretty well."

Having taken drawing classes sponsored by the Works Projects Administration (WPA) during the late stages of the Depression, Golub could draw skillfully, although his figures could be and frequently were deliberately clunky and overly condensed. His early images were more or less

6.1 Leon Golub, *Pre-Columbian,* 1949. Lithograph, 71.1 × 54.6 cm.

based on, or 'stolen' from, primitive and Greek art, distorted and made more aggressive and raw. The prints entitled *Pre-Columbian* and *The Burnt Man* (figures 6.1, 6.2) indicate that primitivism, but eventually he shifted into his more recent style. "I am still trying to keep, if I can, a certain edge to them, and a certain rawness to them. I am not trying to work like some salon painter—more ugly."

Even though the south of Chicago was not a fearful place to work during those early years, the pictures Golub presents today, of black men in quiet dominance or resistance or of mercenaries and gangs, seem to convey some first-hand knowledge of a more threatening society. How does Golub explain this kind of imagery?

You would need psychoanalytic exploration (and then some!) to find out why people make what they make! Obviously a figure which is painted in a smooth way which doesn't show tension; supposedly that person is more at ease in the world than someone whose work is full of tension. Artists who are stressed and tense may pick subjects that are also full of tension, like war, interpersonal struggles, and so on. At the same time, you realize that it doesn't always correspond. It is very hard to get to the ultimate sources. My orientation is to go toward more extreme situations, and I have tried to choose subjects which refer to situations that are really going on, like interrogations, death squads, and mercenaries—real situations in real time.

There is a relationship between the subject matter Golub chooses and the technical or aesthetic means he uses; his rawness fits the subject. They are not at cross purposes. "You have to start from somewhere and you start from yourself. Let's say people are *obsessive.* You can be obsessive and express this, or obsessive and cover it up. The difference between someone who is successful in art might be that you connect your obsessions to things *outside* yourself. You connect them to a big theme. I think this is true of most artists, although one can never generalize because the minute you do you become dogmatic."

This idea of obsessions has never been clearly answered by Golub. He believes we can discover the answer for ourselves, through his work. The work itself is an amazingly continuous process of an attempt at self-awareness. The point is that ultimately all art, while it is biographical and psychobiographical, a 'psycho-history,' so to speak, gets a very peculiar identity of its own. As Golub points out, if you look at Renaissance artists, it is interesting to know what they were like

6.2 Leon Golub, *The Burnt Man,* 1970. Photo-screenprint, 96.5 × 127 cm, published by Chiron Press, New York.

personally—was Carravagio gay, for instance?—but most people can tell enough of what they need to know from the work itself. Donald Kuspit remarked that "Golub is savagely struggling to exalt himself, to become his own father, and the peculiarly hypochondriac pictures . . . proclaim a frustration of self trying to cure itself through male egomania." [1]

Golub was not obviously a political painter until the 1960s, but rather an artist who was seeking a sense of identity. Perhaps the beginning of his politically active career corresponds to the time when he himself linked his obsessions with things outside. Not only is the *self* threatened, but also the world that contains it. "I think of myself as a realist; people who challenge my work on the basis of its subject matter must be blind, because what goes on in the world is much worse than what I

show." Golub's work is a critique of society, with a strong emphasis on the aggressor, not the victim. "Victims are always humanized by their victimization. That is the only state allowed them. They are always in a restricted, psychic stance, one of suffering and pain. Everything else has been removed from them, whether in art or in real life" (see figure 6.3).

In many ways victims represent wounded selves. They can be destroyed, lose their freedom, but still remain symbols of *spirit,* always in a tortured state, but able to offer spiritual resistance. Their aggressors, on the other hand, are humanized—they do not seem so unlikely. They can be smiling, while the victim cannot. They can be jovial, blasé, even sexual. "You can show camaraderie, a guy 'thumbs up,' even drinking a beer, but you can never show the victim this way.

Leon Golub and Nancy Spero \ 61

6.3 Leon Golub, *White Squad (III)*, 1982. Acrylic paint on linen, 304.8 × 436.9 cm, published by Chiron Press, New York.

6.4 Leon Golub, *Double Winged Sphinx*, 1972. Silkscreen, 96.5 × 127 cm, published by Chiron Press, New York.

6.5 Leon Golub, *Winged Sphinx II* 1972. Silkscreen, 127 × 96.5 cm.

6.6 Leon Golub, *WorldWide,* 1991. Installation view, Brooklyn Museum Grand Lobby.

6.7 Leon Golub, *WorldWide,* 1991. Installation view, Brooklyn Museum Grand Lobby.

The victimizers can be mixed up, *they* can be obsessed, they can be capable of generosity among themselves. A guy can go on a killing binge and steal a toy and bring it back and give it to his child and enjoy the pleasure. So in a sense, you have more leeway, curiously. There is a greater range of expression permitted."

This emphasis on the aggressor enhances the feeling of power—male power—that is the foundation of Golub's work. The figures become 'warriors'; they acquire a patriarchal identity. Without his identifying it as such, Golub likely alludes to his possible 'unconscious obsession'; that is, the loss of his father when he was twelve years old. His use of the sphinx image (figures 6.4, 6.5), a monstrous hybrid, half-animal, half-human, was an earlier attempt to deal with these obsessions within the self. His current work has encompassed that self and overpowered it by sheer size and weight, yet its vulnerable layers of 'skin' are exposed through the scraping technique.

As the work of any successful artist progresses through stages, Golub's style, which began with the historical layering of his early prints and evolved into the physical layers of his painting style, reflects further evolution in the 1991 installation *WorldWide* (figures 6.6, 6.7), in the grand lobby of The Brooklyn Museum, and in a later in-

6.8 Leon Golub, *White Squad*, 1987. Lithograph, 73.7 × 104.1 cm, published by Rutgers Center for Innovative Printmaking, Rutgers University, New Jersey.

stallation at the Museum of Contemporary Art in Montreal. Golub's work in those locations marked a departure from his traditional mark making into a world of transparency. Viewing these installations became a field experience. The viewer walked through half a dozen different images, some, distorted photo transparencies taken from his paintings, others taken from news photographs. The overlapping or layering allowed many viewing points, as well as points of view.

The manipulation of photo transparencies is not new to Golub, since many of the prints he has produced in the last six or seven years have used photo processes, usually images taken from paintings, like *White Squad* (figure 6.8). The intriguing qualities of the distorted photo footage has surfaced in a few recent paintings. "In some of the paintings I have done in recent years, say four

or five years, I try to show shifting perspectives and break up the forms, so the figures are half-glimpsed, distorted, and light moves through them." The progression to six-foot photographic-film installations is a natural path for an artist who is continually searching. The scraped paintings mimicked the brutality of the early prints, and now the layered transparency installations are physically becoming the 'skin' of our collective reality.

In the early 1970s, women artists realized the extent to which art was 'gendered.' Coming to understand the idea of the male 'power play' or the idea that "great" works of art are produced by white men encouraged women artists to become aware of their marginalized status and to

6.9 Nancy Spero, *Swastikas*, 1968. Gouache collage on paper, 63.5 × 86.4 cm.

insist on their own identity. Women artists during the 1950s and early 1960s sought to "degender" art in order to compete in the male-dominated, mainstream art world. Nancy Spero was active in WAR (Women Artists in Revolution) in New York (1969–70), which encouraged feminist publications, exhibitions, and institutions, such as the gallery A.I.R., where she exhibited in the 1970s.

About the A.I.R., Spero says:

Because we paid our own way at A.I.R., there was no gallery director or owner, we were each responsible for our own shows. I had long been independent in terms of choice in what I wanted to do. I was in my early forties, rebellious, and angry. I had decided never to paint on canvas again (1966). I was dissatisfied with painting and wanted to break through the pomposity of the male-dominated, paint-on-canvas art world. The first images on paper were the *War* paintings, then the *Artaud* paintings, followed by the *Codex Artaud* (figures 6.9–6.13). I would rent bulletin typewriters and type language, then tear the sheets and fracture it even more, and then collage it to the paper alongside hand-painted images. The tension was not to be illustrative but to stress meanings. These images just took off. Later I wanted to change, and I got into thinking about women, and my frustration and anger about the art world in terms of being a woman. The works went from overtly political to more personally political, about art and one's own voice, or lack of voice.

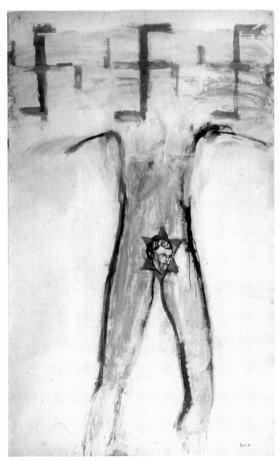

6.10 Nancy Spero, *Bomb with Swastikas and Star of David*, 1969. Gouache on paper, 91.4 × 61 cm.

6.11 Nancy Spero, *Codex Artaud I* (detail), 1971. Painted collage on typewriter paper, 58.4 × 226.1 cm.

6.12 Nancy Spero, *Codex Artaud VI,* 1971. Painted collage on typewriter paper, 52.1 × 316.2 cm.

6.13 Nancy Spero, *Codex Artaud VI,* 1971. Painted collage on typewriter paper, 52.1 × 316.2 cm.

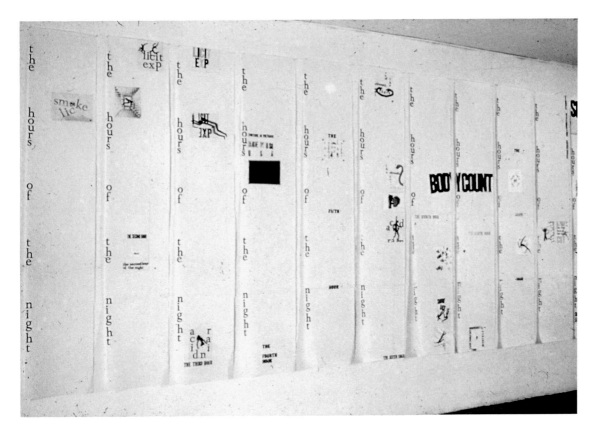

6.14 Nancy Spero, *The Hours of the Night,* 1974. Handprinting and gouache collage on paper, 274.0 × 670.6 cm.

Spero's haphazard 'print' works became controlled happenings. Her extended linear format, an untraditional style of collaged paper panels (either Sekishu or Bodlian), became manifestos. "They were meant to get out to the world, although no one was looking." Feminism called for an expansive approach to art. The use of narrative, autobiography, decoration, ritual, and popular culture helped catalyze the development of postmodernism. Language helped classify Spero's unique identity out of the twisted remnants of family, environment, and past.

The first image with language I printed on paper was *The Hours of the Night,* in 1974, two vertical panels totaling 9 × 22 feet [figures 6.14, 6.15]. I used typography, collage, and painted images for *Torture of Women* (1976), which is 20 inches by 125 feet. It is about the horrible mistreatment and murder of female political prisoners, mostly from South and Central America and Turkey. I used wood-type alphabets and had my images made into black-and-white letterpress plates. I now have over 250 letterpress plates, which are hand-printed in varying colors, rhythms, pressures, etc.

Although Spero has not painted since the late 1970s, she still calls herself a painter. "The only time I draw or paint now is when I am making these images for letterpress plates." Spero's definition of a printmaker is one who makes the more conventional type of multiple printings that form an edition. Spero says that the way successful artists (painters), such as Frank Stella and Alex Katz, use prints today is subsidiary to their 'real' work and that the prints become prized because of the artists reputations. Unlike these artists, Spero chooses printed technology, just as another painter might select acrylic over oil paints for a desired effect; that is, to help convey her meaning.

6.15 Nancy Spero, *The Hours of the Night* (Panel 6), 1974. Handprinting and gouache collage on paper, 274.0 × 670.6 cm.

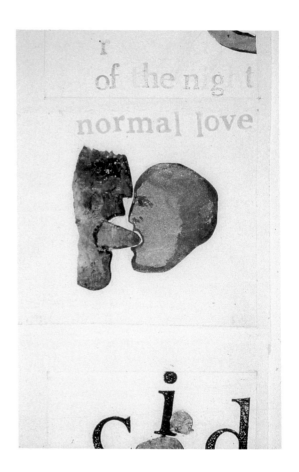

Spero does not make editions. Of contemporary artists using print media today, she is perhaps the only one who is truly using multiplicity to create her primary work. She says: "Leon and I had an exhibition in Salzburg. I had, as usual, variable printed images; now that is my real work. Leon had prints from way in the past. They were not his real work. They are my main work! I call them paintings only because I have been trained as a painter and I have this mental set. Is it an escapist stigma?"

The conscious move away from canvas led Spero naturally to paper. "I think paper is the most flexible supple surface. Supposedly work on paper is less valuable. It just isn't considered as substantial. I love thin paper, I talk about ephemeral—the delicate look of it—yet it is very strong."

Although Golub's spontaneous-looking work (not nearly as easy as it looks) seems impetuous and colorful compared to the earthy delicacy of Spero's, there are many similarities. Her version of the same power, the same anger, the same comment on society, is from the feminist viewpoint. *Picasso & Fredricks of Hollywood* (figure 6.16), handprinted with printed collage on paper scrolls, conveys a social parody on many levels through the juxtaposition of the white male artist and black lace underwear. Images of women pantomime victims. The surfaces of the wrinkly glued areas of the collage on delicate paper could almost represent skin, layers of life, past and present. "I used to say they are like my skin, to roll and unroll; they are

fragile. Even though they are delicate, they have brutal content—bombs, victims, etc."

Spero's elegant surfaces and layering techniques pull the viewer into the work, then the images deliver their forceful blows unexpectedly. "One work I sold years ago was an image of two silvery swastikas on sekishu paper. You could barely see them; and collaged onto that I had eight heads on the tips of the swastikas with Stars of David on their cheeks and the years of the holocaust like tattoos. The woman who was curating bought it for a bank collection quite deliberately. It hung on the wall in the bank for awhile, until someone noticed the content, and then they took it down."

"Women's art is taken less seriously than men's." With this statement Spero acknowledges that 'identity' for women is "socially constructed." She is one of many feminist artists who investigate culture and the self through role-playing in

6.16 Nancy Spero, *Picasso & Fredricks of Hollywood,* 1990. Handprinting and printed collage on paper, 50.8 × 558.8 cm.

her work. "Images recur in my work. The images in my work are like actors in a stock company. They are my main actors and they appear and reappear, each time differently." Her incorporation of graphic language draws attention to a society dominated by advertising, where identities are culturally determined. She 'unvalorizes' the privilege of the patriarchal male's painting and beautiful mark making.

The works of Golub and Spero bring to light current problems of pigeonholing techniques, especially printed media, as separate areas of connoisseurship. Golub, although not considering himself a printmaker, developed his fundamental approach to image through prints in the late 1940s and 1950s. Spero works exclusively in printed images, even though she is in the habit of calling herself a painter. We think of painting as the medium to convey major ideas, yet here are two important artists who have found their voices through prints.

NOTE

1. Donald Kuspit, *The Existential/Activist Painter: The Example of Leon Golub* (New Brunswick, N.J.: Rutgers University Press, 1985), 76–77.

AN INTERVIEW WITH ERIC AVERY

Barry Walker

INTRODUCTORY NOTE

I first heard about Eric Avery's work from Robert Rainwater of the New York Public Library and from Gertrude Denis of the Weyhe Gallery. Of course I was intrigued to meet this psychiatrist/physician who had been making prints in a refugee camp. I have a vivid memory of Eric's walking through the front door of my gallery with a tube of prints under his arm and unceremoniously unfurling them. Strewn before me were a range of images—powerful and raw—drawn from both personal experience and other works of art. Now, some ten years later, this ritual of his bringing his new prints to my gallery has repeated itself over and over. I always look forward to the leaps and changes in his prints, and, more recently, in his print installation work.

Our years of correspondence reveal Eric's unshakeable involvement with human suffering and advocacy for the survivors of that suffering as well as his turbulent battle with making art. In fact, one of Eric's great strengths is his ability to communicate his life as art. Me in '83, *and* Self Portrait at 40, 1989 *(the first with a tear in his eye made after returning from his medical work in*

Somalia; the other, six years later, wearing a polka dot shirt—his father had told him his mother was wearing a polka dot blouse the evening he was conceived—are poignant records of his struggle to express his inner and private life while simultaneously exploring broader political content.

Eric continually ransacks art history and transforms appropriated images, imbuing and underscoring them with personal and contemporary relevance. As a result, his work speaks across the centuries and in so doing evokes the meaning and radical spirit of artists past and present such as Goya, Kollwitz, Posada, Gellert, Coe, and Wojnarowicz. For example, The Blue Bath, 1986, one of the first prints about AIDS, is inspired by Dürer's Men's Bath *and places this twentieth-century plague in the context of history and art history. Similarly,* Massacre of the Innocents, 1984, *makes us look beyond the time of Raphael and reconsider the content as seen through our contemporary experience with war refugees. Here I see a parallel in Eric's work with that of director Peter Sellars, whose production of Mozart's opera,* Don Giovanni, *jolts us into reassessing the dark side of Mozart's opera in addition to the music. In recent works, such as the grand-scale linocut wallpaper installation of marching soldiers at the Boston Museum of Fine Arts, Eric's focus on repetition and pattern create an unsettling force which surrounds us and is at once beautiful and challenging in its ambiguity.*

Eric's intense and innate response and commitment to the art of printmaking has resulted in more than 150 different prints from 1980 to 1994. Ultimately, his multifaceted professional history is not what is outstanding about his art. What matters is his resonant and compassionate voice and the trail of distinct and important images that he continues to make—both for himself and for us.

MARY RYAN
Mary Ryan Gallery, New York

BARRY WALKER: Why did you choose printmaking as your primary medium? Was it because of the references to artists like Posada, or because printmaking is supposed to be the democratic medium, which it really isn't anymore. . . . Why do you make prints?

ERIC AVERY: I don't believe in free will, so I don't believe we actually make choices. I've been making prints since I was a child. I made block prints when I was thirteen and sold them as greeting cards in West Texas. I've been making prints consistently for thirty years.

I made prints in college at the University of Arizona, where I had a great printmaking teacher, Andrew Rush. I was trained in intaglio, but he

7.2 Eric Avery, *Nuclear Wish for Las Dure Refugee Camp*, 1980. Woodcut, 100.3 × 69.8 cm.

told me that my real medium was relief prints. Actually he was the one who encouraged me to go to medical school. It was during the Vietnam war, and one reason was to stay out of the war. I did my medical training in Texas and made art all during that time.

BW: You didn't have to go to medical school. There were certainly a lot of other ways people of our generation could stay out of the draft.

EA: My father was a doctor, and I always had it in the back of my head that I might want to be one, but I was encouraged by my family to be an artist. When I was in college, this preoccupation with being a doctor kept coming back to me. I decided that I needed to deal with it. Rush, who had known me for years, suggested that I take some science courses to see if it was a possibility. I found inorganic chemistry much easier to do than art. If you memorized the rules in chemistry, everything worked. I couldn't find any rules in art. Science was easy for me and I did well. Then I applied for medical school and I was accepted.

BW: Where did you study?

EA: At the University of Texas Medical Branch at Galveston—I'm a Texan. Art is the way I deal with what's happening in the rest of my life. In medicine, even though I loved surgery, the area I was most naturally inclined to was psychiatry.

I did my psychiatric residency at New York State Psychiatric Institute/Columbia Presbyterian Medical Center in New York City. I lived on the Lower East Side. The artists I was living around seemed to be a lot like me, although I was a doctor. It was during that time that I began to identify myself as an artist who was also involved in medicine.

BW: Did you constantly identify yourself as an artist first and a medical doctor second?

EA: Yes. I finished my training in adult psychiatry and began making prints at the Lower East Side Printmaking Workshop. I had made an agreement when I started medical school that I would stop at the end of however far that went. Eight years after I started, I was a trained, licensed physician/

psychiatrist, and I stopped. I stayed in the East Village and joined a street band.

BW: This was an agreement with yourself?

EA: Yes. It was very confusing and traumatic for me to shift out of the mind-set of being a doctor to being a baritone saxaphone player, but it was a great time in my life. For two years I lived with artists on the Lower East Side and made art. It was the late seventies—a great time to be in New York. Then I read about refugees coming out of Cambodia and Thailand who were dying by the thousands. So I volunteered to go help. I felt that it was immoral to have all this medical training and not at least offer to do something, so I volunteered to return to being a doctor to work in that catastrophe.

BW: You had made another decision about your medical career though, hadn't you? Not to practice for money?

EA: Well, I could probably have stayed in New York City, but I decided that if I were going to practice medicine, it would be in a place where I was practicing for reasons other than making a living or to support myself in a life-style that was about just enjoying myself. I loved living in New York, but there were too many psychiatrists. I knew that where I was from in Texas there were very few people who were trained as I had been. In the back of my mind, I thought I would eventually practice there in some way. I didn't have a big vision; it was just what life might be like somewhere down the road.

I did what I needed to do at that time, which was to volunteer as a physician. I ended up not in Thailand, but on a ship that worked with Vietnamese refugees in Indonesia. In one of the abandoned refugee camps, I took apart some of the wooden plank beds, moved the wood to my cabin, and did a whole set of woodcut prints on my work in Indonesia.

I then was moved to Somalia, where I helped set up a feeding program in a camp of forty thousand people. We worked only with starving chil-

7.3 Eric Avery, *Demoiselles d'Avignon de San Ygnacio*, 1984. Linocut overprint in poster, 71.1 × 67.3 cm, edition 5.

dren. There was very little water and very little food. I was the medical director and supervised a team of twelve people. We were feeding thousands of children a day. After three months I was totally burned out and had my first artistic breakdown. I scavanged wood and began making a series of woodcuts. They were very aggressive—prints of nuclear bombs blowing up the camp. . . .

After twelve months in Indonesia and Africa I returned to the United States, to my home on the Texas/Mexico border. I went into counterculture shock. I worked out of that depression in San Ignacio by making work about how I felt.

BW: Why San Ygnacio?

EA: The painter Michael Tracy, a friend from medical school days, had a studio in San Ygnacio. While I was waiting to be placed in Thailand as a doctor, he was away and needed someone to stay at his house. I moved all my things to south Texas from New York City, and it was from there that I went to Indonesia. When I came back to the U.S.,

7.4 Eric Avery, *Death Gives Birth to Beauty*, 1982.
Linocut, 105.4 × 76.2 cm., edition 20.

Michael helped me get refocused on my artwork.
I just stayed in San Ygnacio and didn't practice
medicine again.

I worked on building my career as a printmaker
and began showing in Texas. Later I took my work
to New York and showed it to Bobby Rainwater,
at the New York Public Library. He suggested
that I show it to Mary Ryan, and she took it on.
I began showing work to other people, and that's
how I met you at The Brooklyn Museum.

BW: Actually I first saw your work when I juried a
show for the Print Club of Philadelphia. I gave it
a prize.

EA: Thanks.

BW: At that time you were overprinting on classic
images that you cut and reassembled for museum
posters. How does that relate to your political
work? Do you consider it all political, or did you
see this as a different branch of your work?

EA: I live on the Texas/Mexico border, so I soon
discovered Posada's prints. I used his skull images,
and that's one of the ways that death became
a theme in my prints. I was making flat relief
prints then, printing them by hand onto Japanese
papers.

Then I had the idea of printing my linocuts on
top of posters. The first reproductive poster image
I used was of St. Sebastian. I printed an image

about the Rio Sumpul massacre in El Salvador that
I had read about, a famous massacre, on top of
the reproduction. The image is of soldiers throw-
ing children off the cliff and using them for target
practice. I read about it after working to save children's lives in Africa. The killing of children really
got me going. My motives are not political. It's
just the way I express the concerns of a life that
does have activism in it.

BW: How do we define what's political—it's a
pretty big grab bag. Those block prints on posters
had a certain exuberance that has disappeared or
been rechanneled.

EA: I'm sorry to hear that, Barry.

BW: Well, your work is very different now.

EA: I was in my thirties then and I was naively
building what I thought was a career that would
lead to an interesting life as an artist. I was in love

7.5 Eric Avery, *Starving African Child with AIDS*, n.d. Woodcut, 35.6 × 55.9 cm.

with the medium at that point, and I still love making prints. I wouldn't have used the word "exuberant," but I think I know what you're talking about. Those were more exploratory images; they weren't as personal as my work is now.

BW: I think that's true.

EA: I've matured now. Andrew Rush used to say that the basic work of an artist is to work on your own life. Your work comes from that life, so instead of focusing on the technical aspects or the promotion of my work, my real effort has been to make my life richer so that I can transfer experience into image making. Your work flows from your life. I've seen a lot of work that starts in the brain and is much more of an intellectual exercise. That's certainly a valid way of making art. . . .

BW: It just isn't yours.

EA: It's just not the way I do things. Considering the history of printmaking, I have identified myself with artists whose work is more activist, more connected. Posada would be an example of someone who sat outside his window to witness the Mexican Revolution. He made it the subject of his work. I don't know if he was out demonstrating in the streets. I don't demonstrate in the streets, but I witness what's happening around me.

BW: You attend a lot of Amnesty International protests, don't you?

EA: Not really. I organize protests, but I don't necessarily go.

BW: Why not?

EA: Well, Amnesty International trained me to be an organizer. So I helped organize Amnesty International USA's refugee work in the South and along the Texas/Mexico border. Three or four years after I had returned from Africa, the Immigration and Naturalization Service began setting up refugee camps around where I was living in south Texas and filling them up with people fleeing the wars in Central America. They called these places detention centers.

BW: Let me get the chronology. Were you in Africa after you were in Asia?

7.6 Eric Avery, *Blood Test,* 1984. Woodcut, 61.0 ×
121.9 cm., edition 10.

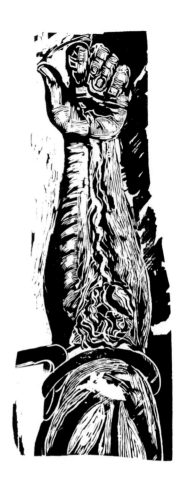

EA: I went to Asia in 1979, then Africa in 1980. I
returned to south Texas from Africa in late 1980.
In 1984 we formed an Amnesty group in Laredo,
Texas, as a way to work communally on the issues
of human rights. It wasn't so much political activism as an attempt to define fundamental human
rights, which is a deeper level of rights than political rights. One human right is your right to have
political rights.

The year I started the Amnesty group, they put
a detention center in Laredo. Eventually we began
working on the issue of the detention of all Central Americans, and detention as an issue in itself.
I began organizing nationally after attending an AI
meeting in Houston. The local members did not
know that all refugees being shipped back to Central America went through the Houston airport.
To me, it was not unlike what I read had happened in Germany. People said after the war that
they did not know there were camps outside their
villages.

When I began to organize nationally in the
mid- to late 1980s, there were over a thousand
facilities, many of them county jails, throughout
the United State that were detaining refugees.
My role has been to work within a human-rights
organization so that other people within Amnesty
can visit detention centers and make contact with
refugee issues, issues of abuse.

BW: Let's get back to the sources of your imagery.
First you were printing on posters of famous
paintings. Now you seem to be drawing more
specifically on the history of prints.

EA: I think there's a recycling of the experiences
of life. The broad cultural context changes, but
you still deal with the same basic issues of birth,
death, sex, living. . . . All those things have been
pictured and dealt with, so there's a reshuffling of
images.

BW: The thirteen basic plots?

EA: I don't know what that is.

BW: There are supposed to be thirteen basic movie
plots that work in various combinations.

EA: Something like that. I once read that Rem-
brandt at one time had the largest print cabinet
in Holland. He constantly referred to them as a

7.7 Eric Avery, *The Blue Bath,* from *Damn It,* 1987. Suite of four lithographs with woodcut overprint, each 59.7 × 85.1 cm.

source of imagery, recycling, recycling. First I printed directly on top of other images. Now I take a historical image and twist it some way. If the viewer knows the source of the image, the print will have another level of meaning.

BW: Would it be fair to say that, in the last five or six years, your work has dealt primarily with two themes: the refugee issue and AIDS?

EA: I would like to say that that's not true but, since you know my work and you're a print curator, your sense of what I'm doing is probably more accurate than mine. Those have been the two issues my life has been organized around.

BW: Which would seem logical if you are consistent with what you said before.

EA: Well, I haven't made pictures of Central American refugees or the camps in the U.S. My refugee images come from my work in Africa. That experience was so traumatic that I couldn't deal with it for years. Then I saw a bowl in a shop in Nuevo Laredo, Mexico. It was a wooden wash bowl that was the size of the dying babies I worked with in Africa. The ribs of the wash bowl reminded me of the ribs of a particular baby. I literally saw the image of this dying African child in that bowl.

I bought the bowl and cut into the interior surface. I inked it the way you would ink a woodcut, then had to figure how to get my paper on this nonflat surface to pick up the ink. I finally used the pulp that I couched down into the bowl. When it dried, it separated from the wood, so I was able to capture the image. It looks like a starving African child. That was the first refugee

7.8 Eric Avery, *U.S.A. Dishonor and Disrespect (Haitian Interdiction 1981 to 19___) State I,* 1990. Lithograph, 118.1 × 88.3 cm, edition 30, published by Tamarind Institute, Albuquerque, New Mexico. Collaborating printer: Mark Attwood.

image I made. It had taken me years to deal with that issue.

BW: So that was your first paper-pulp piece. I assume you liked the medium and decided to continue with it.

EA: I wanted my prints to have a more physical quality than a flat print under glass. I wanted to make prints to have a physical presence to them, and I wanted to print off surfaces that weren't flat. I developed an ability to print from surfaces that aren't traditionally used for making prints.

BW: And you found that traditional printmaking methods did not satisfy this need?

EA: I wanted more dimension. My visual skills are in a fairly shallow plane, so I can't work completely in the round. These pulp pieces allowed me to expand the depth of my work. Also, they don't need to be framed. I can put velcro on the backs and they can be shipped very easily, like egg crates stacked up.

BW: But couldn't the ends break off fairly easily? Aren't they quite fragile?

EA: Museums take good care of art work.

BW: We like to think so.

EA: They're not so fragile. And they do get put behind plexiglas—by the few people who collect them.

BW: Would you prefer they not be?

EA: I'd prefer that they be hung for a while, then be wrapped in cloth and stored away. It's hard for people to live with my work, so these are the kinds of issues I don't have to face. My work isn't widely hung in homes.

BW: So, in a way, you made the same decision as an artist that you did as a doctor—never to do it for money.

EA: I now know that my relation to money is related to my class background. Sue Coe helped me become conscious of class; I didn't know anything about it.

BW: Your father was a doctor?

EA: My father was a doctor and his father was wealthy. Money was always around for me, so I never really understood what you have to do in order to make money. I've been able to support myself selling my art, but it just happened. I never had a strategy. I am going to practice medicine now for money.

BW: But to support your career as an artist, right? Not to join a country club.

EA: I do have to support myself as an artist. I am, of course, going to continue making art. I think it will be much more interesting. My ultimate goal is to make a suite of prints that has some relation to Goya's *Disasters of War*. I believe that the part of my life that I'm moving into now will lead to a set of prints that will capture this time of AIDS in our society and culture.

BW: What exactly are you going to do?

EA: I'm taking a fellowship in AIDS psychiatry at the hospital of my old medical school in Galveston, to develop their in-house AIDS services. I'll be focusing on the interface of psychiatry and medicine, so I'll be working on a border again. I'll be working with the AIDS team in the university hospital, developing a program within the Department of Psychiatry to address this very difficult and unfriendly disease.

BW: How do you see your medical work interacting with your image making?

EA: It has been my experience in the past that it's impossible to do two things fully at the same time. I will be more active in the medical mode now, so I think that my image-making productivity will definitely decrease.

7.9 Eric Avery, *Summer Boogie Woogie*, from *Damn It*, 1987.

BW: But your work with AIDS patients will affect your imagery?

EA: I'm trying now to work with the issue of AIDS, but not to make pictures of the suffering, although I'm sure that will be in my work. There's another strategy that's being used by AIDS activist groups like Act Up. They extend the print medium to include mechanically reproduced images like Barbara Kruger's manipulation of words and images. They use graphics and mechanically reproduced posters. Their strategy is to mobilize people to take some kind of action. I'm now in the dilemma of trying to define how I'll approach that issue.

BW: In your last show in Houston (at Graham Gallery), the first room consisted of images dealing with the Haitian refugee problem. The rest

of the show dealt with the AIDS crisis. In those works you were going far beyond traditional print-making media into what many would consider reproductive techniques. Other than to make the work more affordable, was there an aesthetic point to this?

EA: At this point the breakdown between the fine-art print and the xeroxed image or the mechanically reproduced image seems less important. I'm less interested in the individual print as an aesthetic object. I'd say my sense of aesthetics is changing.

BW: So it's much more than making prints that you can sell for fifty dollars.

EA: That's another one of my strategies—to make the work more accessible. Again I learned it from

7.10 Eric Avery, *Healing Before Art*, from *Damn It*, 1987.

Sue Coe. She has her big drawings photomechanically reproduced to make photo-etchings that are sold for twenty-five to fifty dollars. That's how I met Sue. I bought a photo-etching of *The Rape in Bedford* at P.P.O.W. in New York. I was amazed that it was so inexpensive.

Now, for my major prints, I can have the image photographically transferred to a letterpress block that I can print on my Vandercook press as a multiple that can sell for twenty-five dollars. I've raised money that way to buy three or four plane tickets for Amnesty lawyers to come to Miami to work with Haitian refugees. I've found that even though my large woodcuts won't sell for eight hundred dollars, the small version will sell at twenty-five dollars.

BW: To a different audience?

EA: Yes. My work is not being collected much by wealthy people. But now I can make it available to art students and people who work in museums or galleries. . . . In that Houston show, the photo-silkscreen of me with a condom over my head was bought by a gallery owner to hang in her teenage son's bedroom. That's a place where my work can serve a real function. I'm very interested in finding ways that my prints can work, other than by hanging them above a sofa.

BW: So you're getting away from the print as a connoisseur's medium. You're also moving into a form of installation art, using prints because they are reproducible images. Would you describe the installation that you did in Boston?

EA: It was at the Museum of Fine Arts, Boston. I was included in a show that dealt with the craft of art making and the relation of the crafts to the politics of the artists. The other artists were Anne Kraus, Faith Ringgold, and McDermott & McGough. It was attached to a show of work by Richard Artswager, who is very much into the craft of making objects, but they are not political.

I made a linocut that was three feet by six feet, a repeated image of soldiers, a response to the Iraqi war. I printed on fourteen sheets of Okawara Japanese paper, and we attached them with wallpaper paste to the wall of the museum. We used it as background, hanging some of my other work on top of it. It got me to the next place in my image making. It was the curator's, Trevor Fairbrother's, idea. He had done a Robert Wilson installation a couple of shows before where he wallpapered. Andy Warhol made wallpaper too.

BW: Robert Gober wallpapered.

EA: Right. For me it was very exciting to put my prints in a completely different context. It wasn't the precious object on the wall that print curators like to look at but not buy. This was showing me in a contemporary context for the first time, seeing my work function in ways that it hadn't before.

BW: Transcending the medium?

EA: My technique is relief printmaking. In that show my prints were put into a context where they stood up to paintings on the adjoining wall. There's no reason that prints should be kept in this closet of connoisseurship. I got very involved with Andy Warhol's printmaking during that time. I think he's one of the great printmakers. He silk-screened onto stretched canvas and they got called paintings. Now that's a very clever strategy for elevating your work out of the pit of contemporary printmaking.

BW: Which you find indeed a pit?

EA: Well, there's no money in that pit.

BW: Is that one of the reasons that you are returning to psychiatry?

EA: I was told that if I could paint, my print career would be different.

BW: That's probably true.

EA: There was a whole set of events that led me to the decision to shift from art making to another way of living. One was my dealer's telling me that she couldn't name a single American printmaker who lived solely from making prints. Yet many prints are being made in America, and many of the best and most expensive ones are being made by painters.

I do paint, but I paint with gouache, and I paint on my blocks. Then I cut the block, so the painting is gone. I can't see the point of painting an image on canvas. If you're going to the effort of making the image in the first place, it should be on a surface that you can turn into a print, so that you have a whole bunch of them. That's the way I'm wired. My deepest satisfaction as a printmaker is looking at the entire edition laid out on the floor or pinned to the wall, seeing it all together.

BW: Are you more interested in the actual volume of the work than in the evenness of the edition?

EA: It's not the quantity, because I can get the same feeling from seeing three of the same image. It doesn't have to be fifty or a hundred; it's just seeing the same thing more than once. My body responds to it when I'm in front of it. It's the way I'm made.

BW: If you could have made a living from your prints, would you still be doing that?

EA: That's hard to say because I don't know what that would be like. I could have moved from the

Texas/Mexico border a long time ago, but because of the problems I was dealing with, I decided to stay. I've lived in a rural situation for ten years. I wanted to move to a city, to open a second studio. I needed to find a way to support myself because, obviously, the prints weren't going to do it. I also wanted to integrate the two parts of my life—art and medicine—again. I'm trying to pull those two things together with psychiatry and AIDS.

AIDS is the illness that is pulling together social issues, ethical issues, sex, death. There are ways that people with AIDS can live that support their immune systems. A frontier is developing within the traditional practices of medicine and psychiatry that's beginning to look at the roles of the mind and the body. There are studies being done on music and its effect on the immune system; maybe there's something in the visual dimension. It's a very exciting time to be able to make a change like this. Instead of feeling that I'm being driven out of the art world because I can't support myself, I feel that this is a move to integrate parts of my life that have been separate.

BW: I know that it's impossible to predict, but can we anticipate your sending us visual messages about the development of AIDS treatments?

EA: I'm not sure that there will be anyone on the receiving end of these messages, but . . .

BW: But you'll be transmitting.

EA: The receivers that do respond to my work tend to be in places where money is not the primary issue. My work seems to have a negative relation to money.

BW: Could you sum up your work in a few terse, concise sentences?

EA: An artist who lives his life well usually has a big problem with dandruff. If you watch an artist walk through life, you'll see a trail of dandruff behind him. The more interesting the artist is, the worse dandruff he's going to have and—you know—who wants dandruff?

PRINTS, POLITICS, POLEMICS

Mark Petr

Theoretical discourse about politics and art since the 1960s has generated a resurgence of interest in the impressions that mediated images make in the conceptual life of their audience. References to a society of spectacle are almost as common on network news as in the pages of art magazines. Western society is currently quite conscious of the manner in which social, economic, and political information comes to its audience through a sieve of mediated formats. Moreover politicians and artists have increasingly crossed paths in this land of free speech, contesting the manner in which culture is to be packaged for consumption.

I do not find it coincidental, then, that during this same period a resurgence of interest in printmaking has occurred. Nor is it a coincidence that I chose to use the words "images" and "impressions" in the first sentence of my introductory paragraph. The concern for image and impression in both politics and art boils down to concerns about how to package content. Those versed, even passingly, in the aesthetic appreciation of works on paper are quite conscious of the importance of a good impression to the positive acceptance of an image, whichever matrix system the artist used in creating it. The dual role of prints, as "the democratic medium" on one hand and as a limited-edition commodity on the other, places them at an interesting intersection for contemporary critical conflicts. Deborah Wye, in her catalog essay for the excellent show *Committed to Print: Social and Political Themes in Recent American Printed Art,* acknowledges the vitality and viability of prints as a genre for both aesthetic and political statement, while many of the entries for individual images demonstrate how artists' social and political concerns intersect with issues of contemporary critical theory.[1]

In two previous volumes of *The Tamarind Papers,* Ruth Weisberg has written provocatively about her concerns that there is an absence of critical paradigms for the making, understanding, and appreciation of contemporary prints. She notes, as well, a lack of interest in creating such frameworks on the part of artists, curators, and teachers who are involved with prints. Weisberg's fear is that without such paradigms the importance of print praxes in the wider theoretical debates of our time will be lost. Weisberg's 1986 essay "The Syntax of the Print: In Search of an Aesthetic Context" tentatively lays out the groundwork for a "discipline-based aesthetic," to be developed upon the categories of function, process, and material.[2] Four years later, after the initial foray resulted only in an exchange of viewpoints concerning her designation of printers as "nonartists" in the col-

laborative process, Weisberg wrote "The Abse Discourse: Critical Theories and Printmaking to further the goal of her first essay as well as t chide her audience for not heeding her initial While I take issue with much of Weisberg's co mentary in this essay, I obviously share her be that such critical and theoretical engagement important for our times. To that end, I wish t begin where Weisberg ended.

In her concluding paragraph to "The Abse Discourse," Weisberg notes that certain issues once seemingly unique to printmaking are no pressed in a wide range of contemporary artw in a variety of media: "The relation of the cop the original, the issue of translation, and ques of multiples, templates, and self-degenerating images carried through many reproductions . are but a few examples."[4]

Here lies my major contention with Weisbe comments: after bemoaning in two essays a la critical engagement with printmaking practic in contemporary critical theory, she cites thei growing and self-conscious use and importanc other media without acknowledging that thro these uses, a complex and interesting discussi of theory has grown. The discourse is not abse it is just not where she looks for it, nor is it be carried out by many people whose opinion sh respects. When Weisberg uses the term "prin makers," she seems to be designating only th artists who work wholly, or at least mainly, in ducing fine-art, limited-edition works on pap and who live away from mainstream art areas such as New York.

For her purposes such a restricted usage is relevant on some level, and certainly the art world must not focus exclusively on work created in New York. However, Weisberg's restricted usage of the term *printmaker* will not lead to her stated purpose of a discourse that "should be inclusive rather than one which creates a new exclusivity."[5] What is at work here seems to be an unconscious agenda to restore "printmaking concerns" and their theoretical figurations to the corners of the art world that sustained them during the times when they lacked currency for a larger audience; essentially Weisberg's call is for the practice of "identity politics" for printmaking.

Among the factors that may affect the reason Weisberg and I interpret the same data differently, our generational difference, though it seems an easy answer, suggests itself as predominant. Having come through art and graduate school in the 1980s, when postmodernism had become "the Academy," I am supplied with a rather different, and all too self-conscious, set of assumptions. The major one of these is the inescapable infusion of the political into most areas of life and culture. Another is that the eclectic whim is more interesting than the specialized tour de force.

The collection of syllabi from studio-art courses, which Weisberg cites in the first paragraph of "The Absent Discourse" in order to compare the content of the courses assigned readings, superficially reveals that printmaking students lack exposure to critical theory. Her citation ignores that few if any art schools allow students to escape without courses in media other than the one in which they choose to focus. Art history and studio classes expose students to a range of theories. The range may not be available in each course, but the effect is cumulative. Critical-theory seminars and symposia even became a mainstay at many (most?) major art schools during the 1980s. These factors, combined with the numbers of artists who in the 1980s came to prominence while working across a range of media that suited their usage to their intent, do place "printmaking praxis, teaching, and analysis in a wider critical framework," as Weisberg's essays hope to do.[6] Otherwise what emerges is a political discussion of what group controls the discourse rather than the expansion of an ongoing discussion. The late David Wojnarowicz, an artist whose oeuvre includes prints and photographs, summed up current attitudes in his statement that

> if anyone ever asked me whether I was a photographer, I would say in return: "I sometimes make photographs." I have never been comfortable calling myself anything that would label my acts of creativity because I don't ever want to take myself so seriously that others would then pull out their magnifying glasses and hold me or my actions or the artifacts of those actions up to the ART WORLD criteria of any given medium.[7]

I wish to press on to what seems to be the core issue for Weisberg and then branch out from there. Basically how can those who discuss the role of the fine-art print in the larger realm of art deal with the legacy of "the democratic medium" and the economic necessity and inherent exclusivity of the limited edition?

As Weisberg notes in the body of "The Absent Discourse," it is in the writings of Walter Benjamin and William Ivins that prints are simultaneously heralded for their role as cultural, technological, and political communicators and derided for their loss of primacy as more efficient communications technologies developed. Because of the emphasis on didactic communications by these two authors, Weisberg find that limited-edition multiples are irrelevant to their concerns. For Weisberg this perception becomes a barrier to the development of a critical theory for printmaking. Benjamin's "The Work of Art in the Age of Mechanical Reproduction" does privilege the unique work of art over the multiple, through what he calls "aura." Multiple originals or reproductions deplete the authority of an image by spreading it across numerous objects. At the same time, however, Benjamin suggests that multiples gain aura of a different sort through sheer number.[8]

This strengthening of aura can happen two ways: multiple originals can meet their audience half-way by being omnipresent (the unlimited edition), or they can be more accessible than unique work as commodities (the limited edition). At the same time, however, Benjamin ranks media of multiple originals by their level of technological development and ability to reach a mass audience. For Benjamin's time, film was the pinnacle of art's ability to communicate to a mass audience. In the 1960s this train of thought expanded to include the medium of television and electronic technology in general, through the writings of Marshall McLuhan. McLuhan's book *Understanding Media: The Extensions of Man* of 1964 established him as one of that time's most popular yet controversial critics of Western society and culture, both contemporary and historical. To some he was an intellectual charlatan and to others a visionary prophet. McLuhan's viewpoint owes much to the theories of both Ivins and Benjamin, while the media theories of Jean Baudrillard, whose thought influenced so much of the art of the 1980s, derived their impetus from McLuhan. I think that a consideration of McLuhan's ideas is the first step toward gaining insight into how printmaking functions in contemporary theoretical discourse.

McLuhan's critique of human social structures through their technologies is quite involved, owing much to structural psychologists and anthropologists such as Claude Lévi-Strauss.[9] It begins with the assertion that humans in ancient history were acoustically oriented, lacking a written alphabet and therefore the capability to circulate information on a mass scale. Oratory and storytelling were the modes for communication; both the giver and receiver of information had to be present, had to share the same space. Learning and the transfer of information happened in groups, collectively. McLuhan calls this state "tribal." He views it as the idealized state of a collective unconscious, when individuals relied upon one another and concerned themselves with everything around them.

The ability of humanity to communicate at one remove came with the alphabet and written language, which created the possibility of independent reading and study. When printmaking and then movable type were developed, allowing humanity to communicate in an exact fashion on a mass scale, they changed the social fabric through the collective unconscious. Groups that had viewed themselves collectively and viewed the world in a holistic manner began to separate. The literate had learned the alphabet, which enforced a linear pattern of thought. Information broke down into categories; categories broke down into subjects. All fields of endeavor moved toward specialization. As books became more readily available, literacy spread. With information published in bulk, the amount of knowledge available at one's fingertips became so overwhelming that areas of knowledge broke down into further specialties.

These specialties were tantamount to the mechanization of human thought for McLuhan. This mechanization, through the capabilities of the printing press, led to an even greater mechanization of social and political awareness, as it also led to greater technical means to ease the burden of survival. Printing capabilities enabled the publication and circulation of technical information and diagrams of new inventions, helping to spread the word about scientific discoveries with greater speed, detail, and accuracy than ever before. The great discoveries in physics and other sciences from the seventeenth century through the Age of Enlightenment led to the great inventions of the industrial era. The Industrial Revolution codified specialization with the assembly line. Each worker did a single task, never seeing the entire process to its end. Specialization, then, can be seen to lead to alienation, the dilemma of modern mass society.

McLuhan remained firmly in the grip of a positivistic, modern conception that more technology would cure the problems that increased technology had created. His particular antidote for the ever-increasing alienation of humankind from one another was television. Simultaneous communication around the world through satellites and microwave towers would reunite humans in a meaningful and holistic collectivity. While events have shown McLuhan to have been wrong concerning television's healing capacity for humanity, his "global village" has developed, for better or for worse, in regard to commodities.

The central support for McLuhan's thesis concerning the increasing efficiency of communications media, which was borrowed from Ivins, remains. Printmaking surpassed drawing and painting in efficiency; photography replaced the print; film went further than the still photograph; television supplanted film; computers are outstripping video. Each increase in speed and accuracy of communication causes a change in the human environment; technology moves to its next advance with increasing rapidity. As rapidly as humankind can assimilate information, events rush forward at an even faster pace.

Facing such a pessimistic determinism, McLuhan treats artistic production, regardless of media, deferentially. In fact, for McLuhan, the only way for humans to communicate effectively is through an outdated medium (which explains why he wrote a book to extoll the supremacy of television); otherwise, the gap between the message and the technology confuses understanding. "Art creates an anti-environment through which we can view contemporary society for what it is." [10] Art can allow for different forms of communication and is not necessarily concerned with the transmission of quantifiable knowledge. McLuhan coined the by now cliché expression that "the medium is the message" for a reason. To take the point of view of Weisberg and regard points of view like Benjamin's, which relegate printmaking to a secondary status among the arts—as barriers to be removed—is to miss the point. Regardless of content the creation of a print places art at a crossroads of social, economic, and political concerns. If there is an overt message to the subject matter, so much the better. A limited edition may just be the most appropriate means to address

Western society's reduction of artistic, social, and political issues to economic commodities. Similar arguments may be made about the relation of the copy to the original, translation, and other matters that Weisberg would label as printmaking concerns commandeered by artists and scholars interested in other media. It is the strength of the place to which critical theorists have relegated printmaking that now has artists bringing printmaking concerns into other media. Within this discourse, which involves artists, critics, and teachers interested in the contemporary relevance to society of the various artistic media, will be found the investigations that will determine a way beyond Benjamin's theory.

TES

Deborah Wye, *Committed to Print: Social and Politi-
hemes in Recent American Printed Art* (New York:
um of Modern Art, 1988).

Ruth Weisberg, "The Syntax of the Print: In
h of an Aesthetic Context," *The Tamarind Papers* 9
1986):52–60.

Ruth Weisberg, "The Absent Discourse: Critical
ries and Printmaking," *The Tamarind Papers* 13
):8–10.

Ibid., 10.

Ibid.

Ibid.

David Wojnarowicz, "Do Not Doubt the Dan-
usness of the 12-Inch Politician," in *Close to the
es: A Memoir of Disintegration* (New York: Vintage
s, 1991), 138–39.

Walter Benjamin, "The Work of Art in the Age
echanical Reproduction," in *Illuminations,* trans.
arry Zohn (New York: Schocken Books, 1968),
–21, 235–37.

The following synopsis is based on two of
uhan's works: *Understanding Media: The Extensions of*
(New York: McGraw-Hill, 1964) and *The Medium
Massage* (New York: Bantam Books, 1967), with
ntin Fiore.

. McLuhan, *Understanding Media,* viii.

CONTEXTUALLY LOADED

A Conversation with Patrick Nagatani

Clinton Adams

It is intriguing to write a personal accounting of how I have used my life's time without directed planning but a whole lot of regret and fascination. This comes at a time of questioning, approaching fifty years of living, facing the millennium, and mediocre creative work. The waterless lithographs were a bright spot in the creative endeavor, but not quite the answer or the burning nebula that I search for. I am stuck somewhere between the gaps of my past at the moment. I worked as a grape picker with Chavez in the sixties, I bagged at the neighborhood grocery market. I worked as a toy salesman, I sat in a smoke-filled room at a drafting table doing technical illustration work for the Jet Propulsion Lab, I delivered the mail as a mounted carrier, I built model sets for Hollywood movies, I drove a cab, I served on the California and Massachusetts Art Councils, I taught public high school in Los Angeles, I taught at numerous junior colleges, I taught at the School of the Art Institute of Chicago, I taught at Loyola Marymount University, I currently teach at the University of New Mexico, and during this whole street and academic process I have struggled to make art. The parameters of the struggle became defined with my earning an MFA from the Art Department of the University of California at Los Angeles. At least I now realize how inbred academia and academic artists can be. I am finding that popular culture is my passion. I believe in synchronicity, not fate. I am trying to take my streetwise upbringing from living in Crenshaw and Los Angeles, and readjust my parameters. Somewhere between this and that or then and now, I want to investigate what it is to be living, looking back and simultaneously looking forward at this fin de siècle.

PATRICK NAGATANI

CA: Your recent work has been described as "contextually loaded." How does that strike you?

PN: It is very appropriate. It pinpoints in two words the way in which I work, whether in my recent prints or in other groups of work. I have a way of gathering information from things that interest me: from literature, from a television series like *Millennium,* or from family photographs. I then work to synthesize that information, so as to find out whether I'm interested in making a piece using it. So much is going on— there are so many bits of information coming from so many different sources—that the process requires weeding out, but that is where it begins. I need to make sense of the concept for a piece; at the same time, my interest as an artist is always to

make something beautiful. For a lot of artists who work contextually, the strategy, if you will, is not about beauty—I can understand that—but mine *is:* I am interested in making images that are beautiful, and that also have a sense of information within them.

CA: You spoke of family photographs. Is there an autobiographical current running through your work?

PN: Not in an obvious way. Of course, you can always say, yes, the artist creates it, so the source is the inner self. Before I made these prints— *Katabasis* and the others in this series—my most recent works, the photographs for *Nuclear Enchantment,* examined a specific issue that I felt very strongly about. The pieces pointed to information and sources that related to that issue—that place, that time, that event—and to the marriage of the nuclear industry, of weapons building, to New Mexico. *Katabasis* and the other prints in this series are much more autobiographical.

I remember John Szarkowski's "Mirrors and Windows" exhibition at the Museum of Modern Art some years ago. My earlier pieces were, in a way, window pieces—I was looking at the world as if through a window—whereas these pieces are a lot more mirrorlike. They reflect back concerns of mine—and that has been a challenge, because I think it's a tougher thing to do, and

do relevantly, so that it makes sense to other
~ople, too.

~: What is the meaning of the title, *Katabasis?*

~: Well, it's a loose meaning. It derives from
~e Greek, and its source in my reading is from
~bert Bly's book, *Iron John.* It is about finding
~e's place, about a period of indecision in one's
~e, about not knowing where one is—a time of
~x, a search for identity. I am paraphrasing this
~d adding more than its exact meaning, but the
~rd served to stimulate that kind of tangential
~inking. The titles of all these pieces come from
~ngs I have been reading. I sometimes just write
~rds down, along with descriptions. Later, when
~ making a piece, something seems to say, "Yes,
~t's exactly what this piece is about."

~: So in addition to visual sources there are liter-
~ or textual sources for your works?

~: Constantly. In fact, I would say that non-
~ual sources account for at least 70 percent of the
~cept—the idea—of a work. They inform my
~isions as to how I put things together. And I
~ visual material from the context, from the
~t itself. That is my most comfortable way of
~king. But I find it very difficult to talk about
~se pieces in any way that describes what they
~ about.

CA: I'm not asking you to do that. The content
of the work is what you perceive as you look at
the work; the sources are something else. You can
talk about the sources, but you can't express the
content.

PN: Exactly. But that raises a question for an artist
who is asked to talk or give lectures: How can you
inform your audience about your work? When I'm
asked to talk about my pieces, what I plan to do is
to talk about my sources. Maybe I'll even do readings from my source material—and thus in some
way articulate the way in which I want my images
to work. Such a talk would be very linear—so it
would be weaker, in my mind, than the images
themselves.

CA: Aside from the textual sources, did the image
of *Katabasis* (figure 9.1) begin with the two central
photographs?

PN: The photograph on the right—the picture of
the three children—is of my father and his two
brothers. I wanted to start with that piece, but I
wanted the image to distance itself. It reminded
me of the coming to America: of immigrants
coming to America, assuming an American tradition—a culture—which was important for them
as a means to integrate into American society. The
age of that image and its source—my father—was
important to me, but not as important as the fact

that three Japanese children were dressed in that clothing. That was really the basis for the image.

I found the picture on the left in a flea market. I had been looking for a group of blacks or Hispanics pictured in a similar way: a group from that period in time and wearing traditional Western dress. I didn't want an image that suggested poverty; I wanted an image of a middle-class couple. When I found it, I bought the card, and it became the second image.

CA: So the juxtaposition of these two images began to elucidate the theme . . .

PN: Exactly. I started with two pictures that I knew I would use, and from those—and from the way they were set up visually—I developed the idea for the other images. But I didn't have them in hand. In the process of appropriation— finding and searching for images I could use—I went to the Double Rainbow and bought every fashion magazine in the place. They loved it; I spent a hundred dollars on fashion magazines, and I scoured through them to find the images I wanted to work with. The decisions during that process were either by gesture or by color—hopefully, by both—and then, possibly, by the type of person who was imaged within a particular advertisement. I took more than enough of those images and started to work with them, in combination with the images I had begun with. It became a step-by-step process; things began to

fall into place. The entire image wasn't resolved at any point; there was constant assessment and change.

What interests me about this work is that changes were dictated not only by how images wove in juxtaposition with one another, but also by formal elements. That's where the formal pa[rt] came in. That was the excitement for me as an artist. I had this information; what could I do with it? I was learning both in terms of my own autobiographical reading, and also through the process.

CA: You then combined the photographs with the line drawing that moves across the top of th[e] composition.

PN: Yes, I wanted to use a line drawing, becaus[e] in that way the figures would become anonymous and would represent a class: they're smili[ng] people, they're partying, they're drinking, and they're bedecked with jewelry. What I didn't want to do was to particularize them, or to crea[te] individual identities. Symbolically, the drawin[g] is printed in gold, as a kind of umbrella to the whole image.

CA: And the faces are nonindividualized . . .

PN: Right. I think people in the middle class— and certainly people in the lower class—seldo[m] have more than a general idea of the classes ab[ove]

Patrick Nagatani, *Katabasis*, 1991, 13-run color planograph, waterless lithograph, 60.7 × 50.6 cm, published ₁ Steps Editions, Richard Levy Gallery, Albuquerque, New Mexico. Collaborating printer: Jeffrey Ryan.

9.2 Patrick Nagatani, *Fin de siècle,* Bat Flight Am[
theater, Carlsbad Caverns, New Mexico, 1989.
Chromogenic print, 43.2 × 55.9 cm.

them; they aren't individualized faces—the face
of a Rockefeller or a Getty.

CA: As I look at *Katabasis*—particularly the photograph of your father and his brothers—I am
reminded of Gorky's painting of his mother in
Armenia, which he made many years later, from
a faded photograph that provided a tangible connection to his childhood. I'm sure you know the
painting. Did it enter into your thinking?

PN: Not that painting in particular, but that sense
of tangible connection. Photographs do that: they
provide a tangible memory of a point in time.
I don't know a lot about my father as a second-
generation Japanese-American, growing up during the 1920s and 1930s. I have fragmented information—and that photograph served to build a
kind of historical fantasy; it put me in touch with
my dad as a child. I've probably been reading too
much Bly, but that whole idea of father and son—
the way in which one understands the male past
in order to find a place in the present—seems to
be really important in my thinking today. That
image struck a chord, as a connection to the past.

CA: Your work has been called postmodernist,
yet you spoke of your intention to make something beautiful. The word *beauty* is seldom used by
postmodernists.

PN: No, it's an issue that doesn't fall into the t[
of postmodernist thinking. But I like beautifu[
things, and the challenge for me in my work h[
always been to bring the contextual image to a[
point where the information doesn't force a ne[
for a lack of beauty, but instead turns around a[
almost demands that a piece be made in a beau[
ful way. I walk a fine line, I know, within curre[
artistic thinking.

CA: Your *Nuclear Enchantment* (figure 9.2) serie[
gains a great deal of its force from the fact that[
the photographs juxtapose an essentially horri[
subject—the ultimate horror of the bomb—w[
a very beautiful visual statement.

PN: On a formalist level, an explosion of a hyd[
gen bomb is one of the most beautiful things
one might witness—if you want to witness
such things—but underneath that surface is
the destructive horror. Stanley Kubrick's film
Dr. Strangelove was about that irony and that is[

CA: An irony also seen in photographs of H-bo[
explosions, beautiful photographs, the magnif[
cent cloud rising, until you start to think abou[
what is entailed in them . . .

PN: And in Kubrick's ending, where Peter Sell[
playing the German doctor who has been para-
lyzed for life, is suddenly healed. The nuclear [

has given him a life power; he jumps out of his wheelchair and is healed.

CA: So with your concern for beauty, you really don't welcome definition as a postmodernist?

PN: Perhaps it's just that I'm not accepted within that definition.

CA: In the end, what you are really achieving is a marriage of social concerns with visual concerns and with elements of personal experience and personal memory.

PN: Exactly, and that marriage fits more closely with the process of waterless lithography than with photography.

CA: I agree. Technically, "waterless lithography" is a new form of surface printing—so new, in fact, that we can't yet be sure what to call it. (I prefer the generic term "planography" because the process is not dependant, as lithography is, upon the mutual repulsion of grease and water.) But whatever the name, it is clear that this planographic process encourages, or at least permits, a kind of collagelike thinking, where images are brought together and assembled, rather than created separately.

PN: Historically there have been processes within the medium of photography where artists such as Jerry Uelsmann have put images together. In some of my earlier work, I had interest in that area. I made installations, layering information within the installations; I did work on prints, collaging and rephotographing them. But you are right about the planographic process; it enables the artist to combine imagery with ink and weave information together, using a different syntax. And I have found that within this syntax—within this language—I am able to place things within a much more three-dimensional field. We use flat inks and glossy inks; we use an absence of color; we take the information and weave it together, and, in a sense, it is the *weave* that interests me: the way in which things work together much more succinctly than the two-dimensional way in which photographic images work together.

CA: Now that you have made a number of traditional and waterless lithographs—and given your extensive background in photography—are there images and ideas that you would distinctly prefer to undertake in "straight" photography, and other images that you would prefer to undertake as prints? How would these differ, one from the other?

PN: *Nuclear Enchantment* was a directed body of work, informed by specific research, and the images were constructed in a method that evolved, for me, from years of experience with fabricated photography in the directorial mode. Now that that work is behind me, and now that I have completed a number of waterless lithographs, I am interested in opening up my creative process through a variety of projects. I want to redirect context to be more about connections

within my personal history. I am simultaneously curious about myth and science and the relationship to synchronicity. Somehow I want to develop work that is based upon how ancient cultures can continue to inform contemporary society. Well, that is the contextual side. Within process I am also quite pluralistic. Yes, I am going to do more prints with Jeff Ryan. I am exploding with ideas that Jeff and I can investigate through new pieces. I want to push, and continue to push, the boundaries of the planographic process.

I have a long-range project that may combine and juxtapose "straight" portraits in black-and-white photography and manipulated images. The subject of this project will be the survivors of the Hiroshima and Nagasaki A-bombs. I am also co-producing a PBS television documentary about the survivors. Most recently, I finished working as a consultant and set designer for a feature film called "Wasteland." I designed a sushi bar for this surreal film about toxic waste and nuclear pollution.

I also have several ideas for small groups of color photographs—but where your question hit home is in relation to a series of "paintings" that I am attempting. I am trying to see how extensions of photography can be used with different media. In these paintings I am going to be appropriating images and applying them through mixed-media—photographs, text, and paint—layered within the canvas or primed surface.

These works sound very different, but they all

revolve around photography and the way in which one can use images.

CA: Are the differences partially a matter of scale? Sometimes in the past your photographs have been very, very large, whereas the planographic medium is somewhat limited in scale.

PN: Right. There's a component of scale. I am interested in expanding the size, the parameters of information, and also in the ability to combine large and small sets of information. I have always loved the ability to juxtapose elements in that way. The limited size of the planographs has been a challenge, mostly because I have had to take almost the same sizes and work them out in relationship to one another—compactly. What is interesting about the prints is that because of that compacting, I have thought less about looking left and right or up and down, and more about moving forward and backward within their compactness.

CA: It seems to me that there is a certain density of ideas in the planographs, whereas in the large photographs—I won't call them photocollages, but they're not straight photographs; they're manipulated photographs—there is almost the quality of a mural. The idea spreads out, whereas in your recent prints it is concentrated so densely that it commands our attention.

PN: I really like that word *dense*, because, yes, the images are both visually dense and—back to that word—contextually dense. There are times in artists' lives—in their perception of life and work—when there is an urge to simplify: when one wants to take an idea and work it out. But I have been in this strange place where I had these medieval things coming at me, and it seems that I wanted to make *dense* work, and it all fell in place, wonderfully, while I was working on these prints with Jeff Ryan.

CA: Before working with Ryan, you made a lithograph at Tamarind. Was that your first experience with printmaking, other than photography?

PN: Yes.

CA: Having made these extraordinary planographs—or, if you prefer, waterless lithographs—is there anything that might cause you to go back to traditional lithography?

PN: Possibly. I like the way the stone provides an ability to direct the mark, and I am interested in that for future combination with waterless lithographs. I think the planographic process (as I am using it) can run a fine line close to the echo of offset posters. What I mean by this is that I am interested in maintaining the mark—or the authorship of the mark—along with all the subjective meanings that the mark can set up contextually. Thus

9.3 Patrick Nagatani, *Canandaigua*, 1992, waterless lithograph, 61 × 50.8 cm, published by 21 Steps Editions.
Collaborating printer: Jeffrey Ryan.

far in the waterless lithographs, I have worked on mylar. On the last piece that Jeff and I did, *Canandaigua* (figure 9.3), I scratched and drew in a kind of imprecise way. I know I would have a lot to learn if I were to draw on stone, but I am interested. I certainly respect artists who have successfully drawn their work on stone; I am constantly looking at lithography and its potential for me.

CA: The waterless process has an ability to bring together photographically generated images and hand-drawn images with an ease that the other printmaking processes don't have. All of them can do it, but this process does it with considerable ease—and, of course, with a tremendous visual richness because of the ability to layer dense inks one over another.

PN: I agree. It also provides me with an opportunity to print images with fantastic resolution of detail. I think this comes closest to the language of photography. I like the way the photographic image is read as a photographic image, with all of the object quality, and with the contextual reading intact. This, along with the density of inks and the ability to layer, makes the process conceptually and aesthetically enticing. And isn't this where we started our interview?

21 STEPS

A New Printmaking Aesthetic

Jeffrey Ryan

I cannot imagine ever meeting a print connoisseur who would not jump at the opportunity to learn more about printmaking processes. Process is, after all, the essence of printmaking. It informs the prints we make, admire, and collect. Within the collaborative printmaking tradition, we master printers are compelled to "discover" new technology. On behalf of our artists, we study processes and their specific materials, hoping to isolate unique visual and working properties. Processes themselves are often called "tools" or "instruments." As screws require screwdrivers, our artists' ideas and visual goals warrant specific printmaking processes. The master printer's study of printing technology is a quest for knowledge, rooted in the desire to match process to project. Print collectors, dealers, curators, and general admirers learn about process and print quality, hoping to support that ideal.

Waterless lithography is a new tool in the original printmaking field. It is the primary medium for collaborative original printmaking at 21 Steps, my workshop in Albuquerque. I began researching all aspects of this medium in 1987 at Tamarind

Institute. The present essay describes this new tool and how it uniquely contributes to the original printmaking tradition.

I begin by comparing waterless lithography to its closest relative, traditional lithography. Both are planographic processes. This means that ink-receptive (image) and ink-rejecting (non-image) information exists on the same level plane. In traditional lithography water, intermittently sponged onto the plane, collects on the nonimage, where it acts like a barrier, rejecting ink from the printer's oil-based-ink–covered roller. Those areas not covered by water (the image) accept ink. In waterless lithography, traditional lithography's dampening phase has been eliminated. Instead of being covered by water, the nonimage portions on the plane are covered with a thin layer of ink-rejecting silicon rubber. Through a mechanism quite different from that of traditional lithography, this silicon rejects ink throughout the printing.

As in lithographic plate making, there are many ways to make waterless lithographic printing plates. There are commercially manufactured photographic plates, methods of converting traditional lithographic matrices into waterless ones, and several possibilities between these two extremes. Since this essay is concerned with process originality, or the potential for a process to contribute unique visual qualities to the printmaking tradition, however, I must say that most of the conversion processes are aesthetically empty. As novelties they may be welcome diversions from lithography, but they do not formally enrich our printmaking tradition. In fact although they produce lithographic-like impressions, such processes are technically problematic and inflexible. Unlike true lithographic surfaces, converted plates are not readily editable. While information can be deleted from the converted plate, permanent additions (aside from scratching the plate to remove silicon) are next to impossible. Given the chance to make lithographic-like prints, I would easily choose lithography over any of the conversion processes.

Waterless lithography clearly makes its original printmaking contributions in the area of photolithography. The technical shift from using water to using solid silicon rubber dramatically affects our ability to hand print photolithographs. In traditional photolithography, the halftone dot, like the stone grain, is always visible to the naked eye. The technical reasons for visible grain size have been removed in the waterless process. The result is invisible halftone-dot printing and the ability to hand print extremely refined reproductions of any two-dimensional visual quality. This ability, unparalleled in hand lithography (excluding offset proofing), nevertheless requires careful scrutiny. How should fine-line reproduction methods be incorporated into original printmaking? And what is to be gained from their incorporation?

We must differentiate between a photolithographic reproduction (poster) and an original graphic made using photolithographic reproduction methods and materials. To do so we must share a particular view of contemporary print originality. In today's diversely technological printmaking aesthetic, what criterion separates the original graphic from the reproduction print?

In my view contemporary original printmaking is an action based in a reverence for pre–industrial-revolution print manufacturing. Although we appreciate the tools, techniques, and inherent painterliness of old printmaking, I believe that the object of our reverence is much more basic. We are fascinated by the hand printmaker's state of mind and try to emulate it. We admire the quality of emotional effort required of our forebears to make every multicolored print before the advent of four-color separation photography, photographic proofing, and high-speed offset printing.

Consider for example the past and present challenge of commercially reproducing the qualities of a watercolor painting. While our forebears studied the original, hoping to deduce an effective set of printing colors, we can scientifically probe it, optically separating its tonality and coloration into a set of four process-printing colors. For the pre-industrial printmaker, the mentally deduced color separations, drawn on and printed from various printing elements, came together on the page to produce a variable mixture of anticipated results and complete surprises. Today's four colors, cor-rectly adjusted, combine to produce marvelous renditions of diverse originals. The printmaking artists/artisans of the past spent roughly the same amount of emotional effort on a cigar label as on a fine-art print. Our industrial revolution, of course, included the drive to design mathematically predictable systems to replace the handmade quality of old print manufacturing. It took about a hundred years, but eventually such systems were the reality behind most of the printed matter (including posters) in the industrialized world.

But the original fine-art print remains an exception. It is here that we eagerly choose the general unpredictability of preindustrial print manufacturing. Like our predecessors we use our imagination and follow intuitions to discover the image through the printing process. So long as we preserve this mentality and revel in the surprises inherent to layering mentally deduced ink-run separations, I believe we can integrate any technique or material (including those used to make posters) into the original printmaking tradition. In light of our technology-inclusive contemporary printmaking aesthetic, this view seems to me adequately open to new technology while effectively closed to plain, industrially generated reproductions (posters).

The incorporation, through waterless lithography, of fine-screen photolithographic reproduction methods into the original printmaking tradition proceeds on three basic fronts: as a form of original photography, as a tool for artists using photographic imagery within larger contexts, and as a tool for artists who do not use photography.

James Casebere's *Prison Series* demonstrates the merits of waterless lithography as an original photographic printmaking process (figure 10.1). Casebere spends much of his time traveling, observing and researching the design process inherent to architecture and objects. From these studies he creates (largely from memory) elegant foam-core models that capture the essence of the observed. The static models are dynamically lighted and variously photographed to produce carefully graphic photographs. Casebere is interested in waterless lithography because it facilitates a mixture of high-resolution and graphic image making not possible in his darkroom. Using four-hundred-line-per-inch tritone (three ink layers) reproduction printing, high-gloss clear and tinted varnishes, and ultramatte ink films, we have learned to make high-resolution ink-on-paper photographic impressions that are more graphic than any of Casebere's photographs. We have developed an exceptionally dramatic contrast range; blacks are fully light-absorbing, whites sharply reflective. Casebere revels in such extremes and in the subtle shifts in tonality and coloration inherent to tritone printing. Furthermore he is intrigued by the sculptural qualities inherent to layering ink films on paper, a physicality not found in black-and-white photography. For Casebere waterless lithography is a new world in which to

explore career-long interests in monochromatic photography.

Perhaps the most obvious and pertinent aesthetic served by waterless lithography is the photo-derived aesthetic. Steeped in the traditions of modern photomontage and pop-art printmaking, and clearly influenced by the prevalence of original painterly prints and commercial design, the planographs of Thomas Barrow, Paul Laster, Patrick Nagatani, and Lorna Simpson are examples of how waterless lithography serves this aesthetic. As an artist with a breadth of knowledge and experience in photo-derived work, Thomas Barrow believes that waterless lithography is "unparalleled in its ability to articulate the photomechanical gesture." His most recent prints, the portfolio *Studio Notes,* uses high-resolution tritone printing to make beautiful photographic images from mundane copy photographs of his own sculpture. He further engages the photomechanical gesture by simply accentuating some graphic element in each of the seven images. In *IV* (figure 10.2) he converts a dark curtain into a solid, ultramatte black flat, the banal two-dimensionality of which thrusts against the careful perspective of the object-laden composition. *Studio Notes* is a study in waterless lithography. It relies so heavily upon the combination of collaborative hand printmaking and high-resolution photolithography that it simply could not exist outside of the waterless process.

Of all the prints illustrated here, Lorna Simp-

10.2 Thomas Barrow, *Studio Notes (IV)*, 1992, waterless lithograph, 58.4 × 48.2 cm. Collaborating printer: Jeffrey Ryan.

son's (figure 10.3) is the most photomechanically gestural. To make this duotone print with text and pigment on coated rag paper, she created the photograph, text, and basic layout schematic. I created the three-hundred-line-per-inch duotone separation, made duplicates, arranged the film according to her schematic, made the waterless plates, mixed a range of ink samples, and sequentially proofed both plates in a variety of manners. The result earns its print originality not through painterliness, but through the fact that the image was materialized through the act of organizing information, making printing plates, and printing one layer of ink upon another. Such is the nature of collaborative photomechanical printmaking. From Paul Laster's colorfully overprinted re-reproduction of public-domain photographs (figure 10.4) to Patrick Nagatani's realistic tableaux using collage, overlay, and drawing to raise questions about magic and the ephemeral (see Clinton Adams, this volume), waterless lithography is a uniquely qualified and generous servant.

This technique is a bountiful medium for artists using photographic imagery, but what about for those who do not? How does this new medium serve painters, graphic artists, and sculptors? As a master printer thoughtfully unfolding a new medium, I am most intrigued by these questions and the challenge of finding answers that remain reverent to the original printmaking tradition.

A painter working in waterless lithography has three general options. First, lithographic drawings on plate or stones can be converted into waterless printing matrices by applying silicon at the point where that drawing would first have been etched in lithography. I have already stated my curatorial and technical discontent with the conversion options. Traditional lithography has survived for two hundred years by doing very well the things that it does; I think it should be left to do its job. Second, color-separation drawings can be made on sheets of glass or plastic film. Known as the mylar method, such drawings are contact-exposed to a variety of light-sensitive planographic plates. Properly handled, such plates are quickly made, very facile, and technically stable.

Many print connoisseurs, fearing the gradual loss of lithographic proficiency, completely reject the mylar method. I have helped artists to make many mylar-method waterless lithographs, with

HEARTLAND HATE SUMMIT

MARINE MAMMAL COMMISSION

Federal Funds

General and special funds:

SALARIES AND EXPENSES

For necessary expenses of the Marine Mammal Commission as authorized by title II of Public Law 92-522, as amended, [$1,250,000] $1,310,000. (Departments of Commerce, Justice, and State, the Judiciary, and Related Agencies Appropriations Act, 1992.)

Program and Financing (in thousands of dollars)

Identification code 95-2200-0-1-302	1991 actual	1992 est.	1993 est.
Program by activities:			
10.00 Total obligations	1,151	1,250	1,310
Financing:			
25.00 Unobligated balance expiring	2		
40.00 Budget authority (appropriation)	1,153	1,250	1,310
Relation of obligations to outlays:			
71.00 Total obligations	1,151	1,250	1,310
72.40 Obligated balance, start of year	234	264	266
74.40 Obligated balance, end of year	-264	-266	-277
90.00 Outlays	1,121	1,248	1,299

The Commission coordinates marine mammal policy and programs; reviews the status of marine mammal populations; recommends to the Secretaries of Commerce, Interior, and State steps to conserve marine mammals domestically and internationally; and manages a research program.

Object Classification (in thousands of dollars)

Identification code 95-2200-0-1-302	1991 actual	1992 est.	1993 est.
Personnel compensation:			
Full-time permanent	529	553	584
Other than full-time permanent	84	103	107
Total personnel compensation	613	656	691
Civilian personnel benefits	86	90	94
Travel and transportation of persons	45	60	65
Rental payments to GSA	71	82	103
Communications, utilities, and miscellaneous charges	37	43	46
Printing and reproduction	22	30	35
Other services	247	257	241
Supplies and materials	14	21	23
Equipment	16	11	12
Total obligations	1,151	1,250	1,310

Personnel Summary

	1991 actual	1992 est.	1993 est.
Total compensable workyears: Full-time equivalent employment	12	12	12

MARTIN LUTHER KING, JR. FEDERAL HOLIDAY COMMISSION

Federal Funds

General and special funds:

Program and Financing (in thousands of dollars)

Identification code 76-0600-0-1-808	1991 actual	1992 est.	1993 est.
Program by activities:			
10.00 Total obligations	299	300	700
Financing:			
25.00 Unobligated balance expiring	1		
40.00 Budget authority (appropriation)	300	300	700
Relation of obligations to outlays:			
71.00 Total obligations	299	300	700
72.40 Obligated balance, start of year	61	49	54
74.40 Obligated balance, end of year	-49	-54	-140
90.00 Outlays	311	295	614

The Martin Luther King, Jr. Federal Holiday Commission was created by Public Law 98-399, on August 27, 1984. The Commission's mandate is to encourage appropriate ceremonies and activities throughout the United States relating to the first observance of the Federal legal holiday honoring Martin Luther King, Jr., which occurs on the third Monday in January each year. The Commission's forty (40) members are also charged with providing advice and assistance to Federal, State, and local governments and to private organizations with respect to the observance of each holiday. The Commission is authorized to conduct its activities until April 20, 1994.

Object Classification (in thousands of dollars)

Identification code 76-0600-0-1-808	1991 actual	1992 est.	1993 est.
11.1 Personnel compensation: Full-time permanent	95	195	367
12.1 Civilian personnel benefits	23	35	80
21.0 Travel and transportation of persons	65	47	75
23.3 Communications, utilities, and miscellaneous charges	11		28
24.0 Printing and reproduction	10		10
25.0 Other services	88	23	128
26.0 Supplies and materials	7		8
31.0 Equipment			4
99.9 Total obligations	299	300	700

Personnel Summary

	1991 actual	1992 est.	1993 est.
Total compensable workyears: Full-time equivalent employment	4	5	8

MERIT SYSTEMS PROTECTION BOARD

Federal Funds

General and special funds:

SALARIES AND EXPENSES

(INCLUDING TRANSFER OF FUNDS)

For necessary expenses to carry out functions of the Merit Systems Protection Board pursuant to Reorganization Plan Numbered 2 of 1978 and the Civil Service Reform Act of 1978, including services as authorized by 5 U.S.C. 3109, rental of conference rooms in the District of Columbia and elsewhere, hire of passenger motor vehicles, and direct procurement of survey printing, [$23,361,000] $24,884,000, together with not to exceed [$1,850,000] $1,950,000 for administrative expenses to adjudicate retirement appeals to be transferred from the Civil Service Retirement and Disability Fund in amounts determined by the Merit Systems Protection Board. (Independent Agencies Appropriations Act, 1992.)

Program and Financing (in thousands of d...

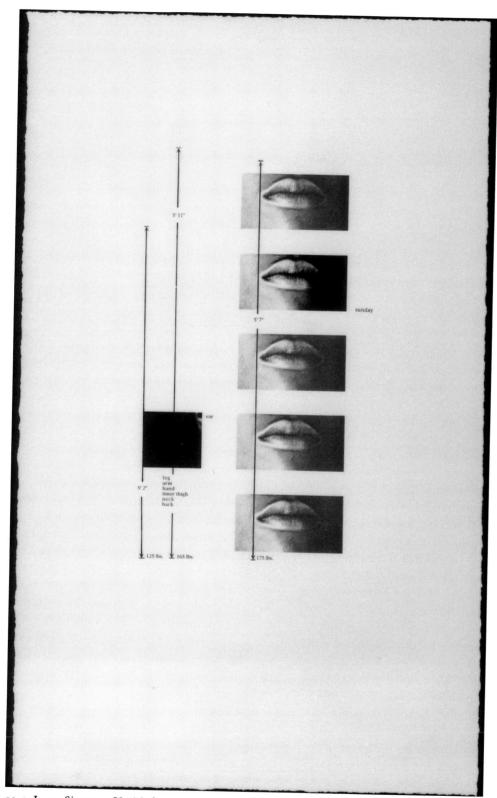

10.3 Lorna Simpson, Untitled, 1992, waterless lithograph, 61.0× 50.8 cm, published by 21 Steps Editions. Collaborating printer: Jeffrey Ryan.

mixed results; my feelings toward the method vary from project to project. For Frank Romero, painter, sculptor, and regular collaborator at 21 Steps, mylar methods are successful where traditional lithography is deficient. He is a prolific painter who revels in the joyous flow of applying paint to the surface. While bogged down by lithography's technical linearity, Romero especially benefits from the speed and flexibility of mylar methods. The opportunity to draw, expose plates, redraw, reexpose the plates, reverse the image, etc., from a single film drawing in rapid succession is more reflective of his painterly working manner. Over the course of some twenty-five mylar-method prints, we have streamlined systems that allow for up to ten-color runs of proofing (from mental conception, through color separation drawings, plate making, and multicolored proofing) in a single day. This painterly spontaneity, evident in most of his mylar-method prints, is the best argument for the mylar method. However, in support of the method's critics, I too am unwilling to accept into the original-printmaking tradition any mylar-method print that merely reiterates traditional lithographic-print qualities. Mylar-method waterless lithography, like traditional lithography, remains a thoughtfully directed option at 21 Steps.

The final and most aesthetically bountiful painterly option in waterless lithography is predicated upon a method widely used in contemporary original serigraphy. In an effort to break with the customary hard-edged, flat, and heavy look of silkscreen prints, many serigraphers are inviting artists to make mentally deduced color-separation drawings on surfaces other than the screen itself. Let us suppose, for example, that an artist making a multicolored serigraph wants the final run to have the qualities of pastel stylus on sandpaper. In the new screen shop, the artist is given a black pastel stylus and a piece of sandpaper, and the required drawing is made in registration to the previously printed runs. It is then photographically transferred through a variety of possible methods to the screen. The result is a very satisfying multiplication of the artist's conception for the final run. Most likely this particular visual quality would not have been as effectively achieved through working on film or directly on the screen. In this example, unique visual goals have been met through a positive incorporation of photomechanical methods and materials into the original printmaking tradition. We at 21 Steps now invite our artists to work in a similar manner. Using invisible, high-resolution halftone-dot printing, they can bring into the original painterly print visual qualities not possible in traditional or mylar-method lithography.

I have presented a brief outline of the ways waterless lithography diversely caters to a broad range of artistic sensibilities. I hope that this essay can function as a foundation upon which to construct a curatorial understanding of waterless lithography. As print connoisseurs, we are all

gatekeepers to the original-printmaking tradition. We must monitor an honor system historically convoluted by dishonest practitioners. The only way to effectively expose improprieties and applaud exemplars within the tradition is to keep learning about process and print quality. Unfortunately I cannot reproduce here those waterless-lithographic-print qualities that I extol. Such is the nature of our connoisseurship; we must foray into the printshop, exhibition, and library to savor our delicacies. Eventually such sources will hold original waterless lithographs from 21 Steps and elsewhere. For the present, I hope at the very least that you have been intrigued enough by this essay to keep asking to see them.

A BRIEF GUIDE TO SILIGRAPHY

(Waterless Lithography)

Veda Ozelle

Siligraphy is a term for the process of making waterless lithographs. This relatively new process operates on the basic principle that ink will not stick to silicone rubber. In traditional lithography moisture acts as an ink resist, because grease and water will not mix. When a lithographic plate or stone is dampened with wet sponges, ink adheres only to the greasy image area and not to the negative areas that hold water. The siligraphic process eliminates the need for water by replacing it with a silicone coating.

Waterless lithography has been referred to by many different names, but not one that narrows it down enough to make it unique to this process in particular. Though "waterless lithography" is perhaps the easiest term of reference, it implies that stones are a part of the process, when in fact aluminum plates are used most of the time. "Planography" refers to any type of print made from a flat surface, including monotypes as well as traditional lithographs, while "driography" or "waterless planography" could mean any printing process which does not make direct use of water, such as block printing, intaglio, serigraphy, etc. Because the use of a silicone solution is central to this process, the term *siligraphy* seems more appropriate than those previously used.

For the artist-printmaker, this new method of making prints holds several advantages. There are no etching charts to follow, no complicated chemical processes to remember, and no ink/ water balances to master. Because there is no need for water, many problems inherent in the making of lithographs are completely eliminated. Without having to fight for a perfect balance between ink and water, the printmaker can focus on other factors important to the success of the image. An artist can draw directly on the ordinary aluminum plate, coat it, cure it, and pull perfect prints in a fraction of the time it would take to produce a traditional lithograph. The waterless process importantly eliminates the need for highly toxic solvents while it provides the printmaker with a fast and inexpensive way to produce quality images.

BACKGROUND

It is because of the commercial printing industry that the concept of a waterless system was first developed. Seeing a way to save money by eliminating the water factor, the Minnesota Mining and Manufacturing Company, or 3M, launched into the development of "driography," a waterless printing method that would be applicable to the offset industry. Research was begun in the late 1960s on the premise that silicone, having nonstick qualities when fully cured, would repel ink just as a thin film of water does in traditional lithography. 3M spent a sizable sum of money on the project, and after a few setbacks they eventually sold their patents to Toray Industries in Japan. Toray has since developed waterless offset plates that can reproduce extremely detailed photographic images. There are now more than three hundred commercial waterless offset presses in operation in Japan, and the small number of presses here in the United States is slowly increasing. All this research and development in the commercial printing industry, however, still leaves the artist-printmaker out in the cold.

It is likely that Toray Industries first inspired the hand printer to experiment with the waterless process. Toray sent some of their early plates to a few art printers in the United States for experimentation. There were two major drawbacks to the Toray plates, however: they were expensive and they required photographic processing, which meant that the artist had to draw an image on mylar or some other material, rather than on the plate itself. A negative was then made from the mylar and the light-sensitive plate was exposed and developed. Since most artists like to work directly, something was needed that would bridge the gap and make this new process more accessible to the artist-printmaker. Unfortunately, because fine-art printing is not a big money-making field, a proper history has not been kept, and it is hard to say who first came up with the idea of mixing a silicone solution and creating a waterless printing plate that could be drawn on directly. As early as 1971, Harry Hoehn was experimenting in New York with "driography." Using the same principles and only slightly different materials, he created multirun color lithographs without the use of water in his process. In 1974 a printer named Chen Lee at the University of Pennsylvania was using similar methods to produce prints. Nik Semenoff of Saskatchewan, Canada, has also been experimenting with the waterless process for several years and in 1990 wrote a paper, entitled "Waterless Lithography" (unpublished), which outlines his process and methods.

Perry Tymeson at Petersburg Press in New York seems to be in the forefront of current developments in siligraphy. Tymeson has been researching waterless printing for a number of years and has recently developed a process he calls "Si Litho." He has developed a water-thin silicone solution that is easy to apply and extremely durable, two ink modifiers designed specifically for siligraphic printing, and a staging lacquer that allows a printer to rejuvenate the silicone coating without harming the image. Tymeson now offers a waterless Si Litho "kit," which includes a coating solution (activated by the mixture of three separate solutions), image developer, ink reducer, body additive, staging lacquer, sponges, and various drawing supplies, including toner solution, crayons, pencils, and a marking pen. Both

lithographic stones and aluminum plates (including photo plates) can be used with the Si Litho method. For more information, contact Tymeson at Petersburg Press, 380 Lafayette Street, New York, NY 10003; phone (212) 420–0890 (EST) or fax (212) 420–1617 (EST).

TECHNICAL INTRODUCTION

As mentioned before siligraphy works because of the nonstick properties of cured silicone rubber. Ink simply cannot adhere to its slick surface, just as it cannot cling to the wet surface of a traditional lithographic printing element.

Siligraphy most commonly employs ball-grained aluminum lithographic plates. The silicone solution that coats the plate consists of 100% silicone caulking sealant, mixed with paint thinner or a thinner substitute. Any brand of sealant should work, as long as it is identified as "100% silicone" and "nonpaintable" on the label. A variety of high-quality silicone sealants can be purchased at any hardware store. Paint thinners are very toxic, so a turpentine substitute is preferable. There are a few odorless substitutes available that have low toxicity levels and do not release noxious vapors.

The basic processing steps are very simple (and are covered in full detail in the processing section of this paper). First a small portion of the silicone caulking agent is diluted with thinner and mixed thoroughly. The mixture is then buffed into the hand-drawn plate until smooth, after which it is cured in an oven or on a hot-plate. After curing, the image can be washed out using dish soap and warm water. Once the image is thoroughly washed out, the plate is rolled up and printed just like a traditional lithographic plate, with only slight modifications to ink and printing techniques (step-by-step processing instructions follow the information on drawing supplies). Since silicone rejects ink, there is no problem with the offset of previous ink layers when printing a multiple-run image. As far as image stability goes, the printing ink clings to the bare metal of a waterless plate, instead of to a layer of asphaltum or lacquer, which can be broken down by water. Since there is no delicacy to the printing base, there is no worry of losing an image between the time the artist washes out and rolls up. The washed-out plate can be left for days or weeks, and it will suffer no adverse effects. The plate can also be left at any time during printing, without the special precautions that would be necessary with traditional lithographic elements. Another advantage to the properly coated and cured silicone plate is that the image will not fade or fill in. The fullness or sparsity of the image depends solely on the inking and printing pressure. Because of the absence of water, less ink is usually needed and minimal press pressure is required to print a full siligraphic image.

WATER-SOLUBLE DRAWING MATERIALS

The drawing materials best suited for siligraphy are those that are soluble in water. As mentioned before any grease or wax-based materials are dissolved by the thinner in the silicone solution, causing them to smear during buffing. Drawing with water-based materials provides some unique opportunities that are not possible in traditional lithography. Most water-soluble drawing supplies are available in a wide variety of colors, particularly watercolor crayons and pencils. This makes it possible to draw the image in a color similar to the one in which it will be printed. The ability to make deletions with water is another great benefit of working with these materials. At any time during the making of an image, the drawing can be removed from the plate using plain water and sponges, rags, Q-tips, or even fingers. This allows the artist to either start over completely or simply rework a particular area. Another advantage of water-soluble drawing supplies is their low cost and ready availability. More important, however, is the fact that they are completely nontoxic. The following materials are capable of making tones and marks equivalent to those of traditional lithographic materials and should be available in most art supply stores for about the same prices indicated:

11.1 A combination of water-soluble drawing materials was used to create this siligraphic image, including three types of watercolor pencils, two different painting crayons, gum arabic, and water-based markers and drawing ink, with plain tap water as a deletional tool.

Rexel Derwent watercolor pencil	$ .83
Cyklop Aquarell woodless watercolor pencil	$1.79
Caran D'Ache Neocolor II water-soluble painting crayon	$ .98
Stabilotone water-soluble crayon	$3.49
Artista II Powder Tempera Paint (1 lb.)	$4.20
Chromatemp Liquid Tempera (1 pint)	$3.90
Higgins nonwaterproof ink (1 fl. oz.)	$2.25

The general guide below (as well as the more detailed information following) can be used to achieve the desired effects:

Traditional Lithographic Materials	Water-Soluble Siligraphic Water-Materials
Korn's lithographic crayon pencils #4-5	Rexel-Derwent watercolor pencil
Korn's lithographic crayon pencils #1-3	Rexel-Derwent or Cyklop pencil
Korn's lithographic crayon	Stabilotone water-soluble crayon
rubbing crayon	Stabilotone water-soluble crayon
tusche washes	liquid or powder tempera washes
shop black	
gum arabic stop-out	gum arabic
airbrushed materials	silicone solution stop-out gum or ink/gum

These water-soluble materials can be used together or in any combination to create unique,

lithographic-quality images (figure 11.1). Experimentation on your part will be required before you decide which materials you most like to work with. The pencils and crayons are reasonably straightforward, and the mark you make on the plate is usually the mark you will see in the finished print. Washes and other materials require some special consideration, however. The following brief tips will help you use the various drawing supplies successfully.

Watercolor Pencils

One very important thing to remember with these pencils is to draw your lightest shades a little darker than usual because a slight bit of pencil dust will lift off the plate when you talc the image, leaving your tone just a hair lighter than expected. All pencils may be sharpened with a manual or electric pencil sharpener. Since the pencil material is nongreasy, it will not damage the mechanism of your sharpening device. A full range of tones and strokes is possible with the Rexel-Derwent pencil (figure 11.2). Obviously I have not been able to test every water-soluble pencil on the market, and I strongly encourage you to find and test new ones. When searching for pencils, keep in mind that a softer drawing material will adhere better to the plate.

11.2 The Rexel Derwent watercolor pencil is capable of a full range of tones and strokes as well as smooth gradations. It has the ability to make soft, light shades and bold, dark lines. If used with water it creates a softer, muted line or a wash.

11.3 The Schwan Stabilotone water-soluble crayon pencil can produce an extremely wide variety of marks. It is capable of making excellent dark, rich tones and can also be used with water to create soft, fuzzy lines.

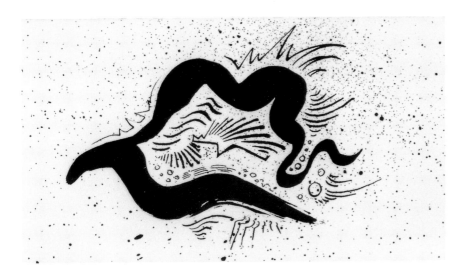

11.4 Gum arabic creates black flats and solid lines and can be used straight out of the bottle. It can be spattered, brushed, or drawn on with a pen and nib.

Water-Soluble Crayons

The Schwan-Stabilotone crayon (which comes in the form of a large pencil), and the Caran D'Ache Neocolor II painting crayon are both available at most fine-art stores. The Stabilotone crayon is by far the more successful of the two, with its ability to make an extremely wide variety of marks, similar to the range from Korn's lithographic crayons #00 to #5 (figure 11.3). The marks made by this crayon are very predictable, and there is virtually no smearing during processing. A unique characteristic of the Stabilotone is that it can be applied with a chamois or lint-free cloth, to produce a look that is similar to lithographic rubbing crayon. The Caran D'Ache crayon is much softer, which causes it to smear a little during buffing. If you talc the image thoroughly and buff the silicone delicately, you can effectively reduce smearing problems. Another drawback to the Caran D'Ache is that it does not work well as a rubbing crayon; delicate areas tend to fill in because the soft drawing material gets rubbed deep into the grain of the plate. Images drawn with this crayon also tend to be a little higher in contrast when compared to the Stabilotone.

Gum Arabic

Solid blacks (or image areas) are created when gum arabic is used as a drawing material. The gum acts as a resist to the silicone solution, protecting the bare metal of the plate from its effects. It is ready to be drawn with as is and will give rich, full flats and perfect solids. The gum can be brushed on, spattered on, or drawn on with pen and nib (figure 11.4). Gum arabic can also be used with technical pens, as long as you clean the pens thoroughly with warm water after use. If you are in search of a less viscous solution with which to draw, the gum can be diluted with water. Be sure to keep the ratio above two parts gum to one part water, or the solution will not be strong enough to resist silicone during buffing.

Tempera Powder

There are two very important things to remember when using tempera powder. First, your image *must* be cured with heat. If it is allowed to dry naturally, the powder will remain loose on the surface of the plate and will be disrupted when the image is dusted with talc. It is preferable to use a hand-held dryer so that you can cure your washes at various times throughout the making of your image as well as control the speed at which they

11.5 Tempera-powder washes may be applied with a brush. Distilled water and a little dish soap were used to make up the wash solution. The washes were heat-cured with a hand-held drier.

dry. Second, as with alcohol and toner washes, a dissolving agent like dish soap or Kodak photo-flow should be added to the mixture. Although tempera powder dissolves fine in water on its own, the soap helps the pigment to adhere to the plate smoothly and evenly by reducing surface tension. Only a tiny bit is needed, but the soap is very important to the success of your image. Unfortunately, if you add too much, your washes will bleed. It is a good idea to have an extra plate around to test your solution on. If there is too little soap in the solution, you will be able to remove the dust with your finger or a rag after the wash is cured with heat. If too much soap is present, your washes will run, travel, and bleed before they even have a chance to dry.

There are two basic ways to apply tempera powder and each creates quite different effects. The first is the wash method, with which lithographers are already familiar. Washes are created by mixing the tempera solution with different amounts of water and puddling it on the surface of the plate. Water retention will allow you to control how and where the washes are laid down, and they will not travel unless you use too much water, have too much soap in your solution, or are careless with your drying technique. Washes created with powdered tempera pigment are quite similar in appearance to traditional tusche washes, having unique reticulation patterns and gradations (figure 11.5). Dry each set of washes thoroughly before laying down the next. Just as with lithographic washes, the more layers you put down, the darker your image will be.

The second way to apply the tempera powder gives more of a "toner" effect, similar in appearance to the soft, dusty images that can be achieved with Xerox toner. Using very little water, the powder can be moved around the plate with fingers, brushes, sponges, Q-tips, or rags. Instead of reticulated washes there will be finger marks, brush strokes, or fuzzy, cloudy areas. The powder can be dusted directly onto the plate and the water added as the artist draws, or solutions may be mixed ahead of time. This method is very similar to finger painting, and there are no particular rules. The only important things to remember are always to use a soap-and-water mixture and to be sure to cure the image areas with heat.

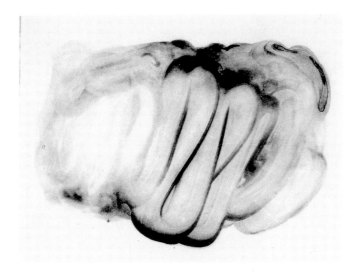

11.6 Liquid tempera used with a little distilled water and dish soap created "toner" effects. The solution was applied directly to the plate, manipulated manually, and then cured with the heat of a hand-held dryer.

11.7 This airbrushed image was made with gum arabic as the spray material. Mylar masks were used to create white areas.

Liquid Tempera

As with tempera powder, there are two basic ways to apply liquid tempera. One produces washes and the other "toner" effects. Liquid tempera should be used with dish soap or Kodak photo-flow in the water and cured with heat, just like tempera powder. Liquid tempera washes are much smoother than powder washes and some very nice, soft grey tones can be achieved, but darks tend to become very dark, and the pigment likes to build up around the edge of the washes, creating an outline effect. The drying of the washes is also much harder to control, although some interesting effects can be achieved. Liquid tempera washes are a little less predictable,

and layering them tends to create more contrast. For toner effects, however, liquid tempera is the best performer. The smaller pigment grains help produce a softer, dustier look (figure 11.6). The gradations are smoother, with less grainy contrast than in a tempera-powder image.

Spray Materials

Gum arabic is the best material for use with an airbrush (figure 11.7). Drawing inks are too thin; they spray unevenly and tend to bleed when they come in contact with the plate. Tempera powder clogs the airbrush mechanism very quickly with its tiny grains, and liquid tempera, when sprayed,

11.8 A water-based brush pen was used to draw directly on the plate and then cured with the heat of a hand-held dryer.

is not a strong enough resist to the silicone layer and becomes impossible to wash out. Gum arabic, however, as the perfect silicone resist, creates an excellent image and will not clog up the airbrush, if a little warm water is sprayed through it occasionally. The image dries very quickly and is extremely easy to wash out during processing. If the transparency of the gum seems difficult to work with, simply add 1 part Higgins non-waterproof ink to 3 parts gum. This will give you a visible solution to use without changing the quality of the image.

Water-Based Markers

Any water-based marker should work fine. Brush pens make beautiful lines and are particularly nice to draw with (figure 11.8). The only rule is that the image *must* be cured with heat, if black lines are desired; otherwise a grey, unpredictable line is the result. Dry the image thoroughly with a hand-held dryer, as you would with tempera washes.

Silicone Stop-Outs

Gum arabic is often used in traditional lithography to create stopped-out areas. To achieve white or negative areas in siligraphy, a silicone solution can be used. Dilute the silicone with 60 or 70% thinner. If too much thinner is added, the stop-outs will bleed, and if not enough is added, they will dry thick and lumpy; so make use of a test plate to get your mixture just right. The silicone stop-out works by protecting the plate surface from the drawing materials. When the drawing is finished and the plate is coated, any stop-outs will be dissolved by the silicone solution. Unfortunately, there are some major drawbacks with silicone stop-outs. First of all they cannot be left to cure too long before the plate is coated, or they will no longer dissolve enough to be buffed down. The solution will reach a full cure in a day or two, so leaving the plate overnight is not an option. Also, since the solution cures quickly with exposure to heat, using tempera-wash materials on top of stop-outs is impossible; when the washes are cured, the silicone stop-outs will be cured simultaneously, making them impervious to the final coating. Raised silicone areas will catch ink during printing and leave marks and shadows. Silicone stop-outs are best used with pencils, crayons, or gum arabic (figure 11.9).

11.9 To achieve the look of a lithographic-gum stop-out, the silicone solution can be applied with a pen, toothbrush, or paintbrush and then allowed to dry. Crayon, pencil, and gum arabic can then be drawn over the stop-out areas, as in this example. During processing the stop-out areas will dissolve and be buffed in with the permanent layer of silicone.

Other Materials and Techniques

There are quite a few materials to draw with that are *not* water soluble. Lacquer-based markers (such as Sharpies), Xerox toner powder, and waterproof inks are among the ones that are great to draw with, do not smear, and print beautifully. The drawback is that they must be washed out with solvents, but if this is not an issue, then they should by all means be experimented with. Any of these materials may be mixed with the water-soluble drawing supplies included in this paper. Washing out a plate with solvents instead of water will not be detrimental to the water-soluble areas of your image.

Another drawing technique not mentioned above is the drypoint method. It is one of the only ways to make additions to a siligraphic plate. After the plate has been coated and cured, the surface is simply scratched with a drypoint needle, razor blade, or similar sharp instrument. Any lines made will roll up and print black. The artist must be careful to avoid creating burrs (sharp, raised edges) in the plate with the scratching tool, as this will damage the roller. The lines may be slow to take ink at first, but they should come up within the first five impressions or so.

STEP-BY-STEP PROCESSING GUIDE FOR WATERLESS PLATES

1. In a film canister or other suitable container, dilute six parts silicone with four parts Turpenoid odorless thinner. Mix together until smooth (a consistency similar to molasses is good). One film canister of solution should coat two $15'' \times 25''$ plates. Put an air-tight lid on your container and save the rest of the solution for future plates; with minimal air contact, it should last overnight.
2. There is no need to talc your image, unless you are nervous that something will smear.
3. Use approximately one teaspoon of silicone solution for every square foot of plate surface, and begin spreading it around the borders of your plate.
4. Using a *synthetic* sponge, move the solution carefully around the plate borders and into your image—do not scrub it into the plate, just move

11.10 The water-soluble materials that make up the original drawing on this plate are being carefully washed out with warm water and dish soap. The plate will then be inked and printed similarly to a traditional lithograph, with only slight modifications in press pressure and printing ink.

it around gently! Be sure to cover the *entire* surface of the plate. If you have areas that are stopped-out with silicone, make sure they are dissolved before you start buffing.

5. Form two buffing pads out of toilet tissue or lint-free Kimwipes. With the first pad, pick up the excess solution until a workable coating is left. Take the second pad and buff gently until the surface of the plate is smooth (hold it up to the light to make sure the coat is relatively even). Keep changing the buffing surface of your pad until the coating is satisfactory, and be sure to wipe away any lint or crud. A medium-to-light buff is fine, and one coat should be all you need. You can use the pads over and over.

6. Cure the plate in an oven at 250°F for at least ten minutes. There is no danger of overcuring your plate, but if you undercure it, the coating will not be mature enough to repel ink.

7. Attach your plate to the press or backing element. Use warm water with dish soap on a piece of synthetic sponge to carefully wash out the image (figure 11.10). Do not scrub, especially in the non-image areas! Although the silicone layer is cured, it can still be damaged if you rub away at it with too much force. There will be a slight stain left in the plate from some of the drawing materials, but do not try to get rid of it completely, or you will end up damaging your image. Most materials will lift quickly, especially gum arabic and markers, but the washes take a little more patience. Using dish soap will coax the more difficult materials to

release more quickly. Washing-out is a delicate task, for if you are too vigorous you will damage the image as well as the coating. If you are not thorough enough, however, some areas may not take ink when the time comes to roll up. As long as you DO NOT SCRUB you will probably be fine; it just takes a few times to get the hang of it!

8. When your plate is thoroughly washed out, fan or blow-dry until absolutely *all* the moisture is gone (do not use cloths or tissues, as they will contaminate the plate with lint and fuzz). You are now ready to roll up and print!

INKS AND INK MODIFIERS

One of the biggest differences between siligraphy and traditional lithography is in the selection and modification of inks. Stiff inks with low grease content and high tack are best suited for siligraphic printing. Daniel Smith Classic Black or Graphic Chemical's Senefelder Crayon Black require the least amount of modifying and give nice full impressions. Any inks with a very high grease content should be avoided. Color inks are much harder to deal with than black inks, and some are just too greasy to work with at all, requiring so much modification that it would be to the artist's advantage just to select another ink altogether. The Flint Ink Company of Ann Arbor has recently developed a small line of waterless offset inks that may be a promising alternative because of their

low grease content and very high tack. The Gans Ink Company in California has also developed a soy-based waterless offset ink. Both companies welcome calls for information or samples; Flint: (313) 995–3100 (EST), Gans: (213) 264–2200 (PST). Although the only colors available so far are yellow, red, blue, and black, many beautiful colors can be mixed with them, and they generally require no modification. I have found that they work even better when combined with traditional lithographic inks, a good recipe being one part waterless offset ink to one part lithographic ink to one part varnish. As far as using only traditional lithographic inks, experimentation is called for to discover what works best.

Ink modifiers best suited for use in siligraphic printing:

Daniel Smith Litho Varnish #8	1 pt.	$11.00
Magnesium Carbonate	1 lb.	$ 3.90
Graphic Chemical Alumina Hydrate	1 lb.	$ 3.70
Gans Heavy Water-Resistant Varnish	1 lb.	$ 7.85

Ink modification

Daniel Smith Classic Black: Add 30–50% #8 lithographic varnish and 1 tsp. alumina hydrate. Add magnesium carbonate if needed. This is the best recipe so far, for the ink remains relatively easy to roll out yet leaves virtually no roller mark on the plate. This mixture makes for a very crisp, clean print. Temperature and humidity may require you to modify your ink further.

Graphic Chemical Senefelder's Crayon Black: Add 20–30% #8 lithographic varnish and about 1/2 tsp. magnesium carbonate, if needed.

Color inks: As mentioned above, some inks are nearly impossible to modify into the proper consistency for siligraphy. Most of the Handschy CS-15 offset inks will work well, but try to use only the stiffer ones. Gans heavy water-resistant varnish and magnesium carbonate are the best modifiers to use with color inks. About 30–40% varnish and a spoonful of alumina hydrate should be sufficient; add magnesium carbonate as needed.

PRINTING AND EDITIONING

When printing an edition, the most important factor for success is the strength and ink-resisting capabilities of the silicone coating. It is true that silicone is one of the most durable substances known, but the solution with which the plate is coated is not only diluted with a solvent, but is also buffed down to quite a thin layer. Although the coating will become more and more impervious as time goes on, it should not be subjected to extensive and repeated abuse. If the plate has not been properly coated and cured, the silicone will begin breaking down in the middle of printing, and a tint will become noticeable around the borders or in the negative areas of the image. The following tips are helpful to keep in mind during the printing of an edition:

> 1. Use quick, swift passes when rolling ink onto your plate. This will keep tinting and scum to a minimum.
> 2. Choose a roller that can completely cover an area larger than the size of your paper in one pass. This is very important, for no matter how perfect your silicone coating, and no matter how swift your passes, roller marks at the top and bottom of your plate are almost inevitable, especially when printing in color. By choosing a roller that is larger than the paper, the marks will end up on your newsprint rather than in the borders of your image.
> 3. Use light to medium pressure when rolling. There is no need to bear down on the plate with your roller,

since there is no water layer to keep the new ink from adhering immediately to the previous pass of ink.
> 4. Set the press to medium printing pressure and adjust only as needed. The more pressure you use, the harder it is on your silicone layer. If you are not getting a full impression, add ink to your roller, before you resort to increasing pressure. Since there is no water/ink balance to achieve with siligraphy, ink thickness and printing pressure will be your only adjustments in order to print consistently.

TROUBLESHOOTING

Most of the problems encountered during the printing of a waterless plate will have something to do with the silicone coating. It will either be too thick, too thin, uneven, or contaminated with solvent residue. Most of these problems are easily remedied, but the better the first coat, the smoother the printing will go. The following information will help solve or keep to a minimum any potential problems. *Important!:* Before attempting to roll ink onto your plate after using any kind of solvent, be sure the plate is completely clean and free of residue.

SYMPTOM: Image will not roll up at all, or rolls up unevenly.
POSSIBLE PROBLEM: Image is not thoroughly washed out, leaving a thin layer of silicone to resist the ink when you try to roll up.
SOLUTION: Wash the plate out again. If there is

no ink on the plate, just go back to using warm water and soap. If there is ink on the plate, clean it off first with acetone and then go back to soap and water. The rest of the drawing materials should lift, and as soon as the plate is free of solvent residue and is completely dry, you may proceed with the roll-up. If the image still does not take ink, your coating is probably impenetrable, and you may have to abandon the plate.

SYMPTOM: Entire plate is taking ink.
POSSIBLE PROBLEM: Ink is not properly modified. Silicone coating is too thin or is insufficiently cured.
SOLUTION: Add modifiers to your ink to make it less greasy and more tacky. Wash the plate out with acetone, clean your ink slab and roller, and begin the roll-up process again. If the plate still fills up with ink, the problem is in your coating. Wash the plate out with acetone and put it back in the oven if you suspect that the coating is simply insufficiently cured. If you think the silicone layer is too thin, however, you must coat and cure the plate again. Do *not* blot the plate back with newsprint. Simply clean the excess ink from the plate with alcohol, being careful not to remove too much from the image area. Clean the plate off with soap and water, dry it, and talc the image *thoroughly*. Coat and cure the plate again, buffing very gently, for the ink will smear terribly if you are too vigorous. A little smearing will not damage your image, but be extra careful and try to get

the plate coated as quickly as possible. Cure the plate again, then wash out the image with acetone or isopar. Before rolling up, make sure the plate is absolutely dry and free of solvent residue. The plate should now print without further problems.

SYMPTOM: Entire plate is scumming, producing a tinted print.
POSSIBLE PROBLEMS: Ink is not properly modified. Coating is too thin, is insufficiently cured, or surface is contaminated with solvent residue.
SOLUTION: Follow the same steps as above. If you think that solvent residue is your only problem, simply wash the plate out with acetone and put it back in the oven or on a hot plate to evaporate the residue.

SYMPTOM: Border area is scumming or tinting.
POSSIBLE PROBLEM: The silicone coating in the border area is too thin.
SOLUTION: You must recoat the borders of your plate. Follow the same steps as for recoating the entire plate, but do not talc or buff silicone into the image area at all. Simply blot the plate back with newsprint and clean and recoat the borders of the plate, avoiding the image area.

CONCLUSION

Although waterless printing is considered to be a relatively new printmaking method, the technology which makes it possible has existed for more than twenty years, and I am by no means the first to become interested in and study the process. Siligraphy is still in the very early stages of experimentation as a viable hand-printing method, and it does not yet have the flexibility of traditional lithography in such important areas as making image additions or deletions, color proofing, and—because of the nature of currently available silicone coating—durability of printing surface. It is not a candidate for the replacement of traditional lithography, but it is indeed a unique new process that deserves attention as well as continued research. This article contains enough information on how to get started on your own waterless printing experiments, and I greatly encourage printers and artists alike to set about making their own discoveries in this interesting new corner of the printmaking world. Good Luck!

ABOUT THE CONTRIBUTORS

CLINTON ADAMS, a painter, printmaker, and historian, has been associated with Tamarind since its founding in 1960. He established *The Tamarind Papers* in 1974 and served as its editor until 1990. His fifth and most recent book about American lithography and lithographers is *Crayonstone: The Life and Work of Bolton Brown* (University of New Mexico Press, 1993).

LYNNE ALLEN is assistant professor of art at Rutgers University, Mason Gross School of Arts, where she teaches printmaking and artist's books. She is associate director of the Rutgers Center for Innovative Printmaking and is responsible for an artists' exchange between the former USSR and the RCIP. A Tamarind Master Printer, she served as studio manager and technical director of the print-training program at Tamarind Institute from 1983 to 1987 and as contributing editor of *The Tamarind Papers* during 1986 and 1987.

VEDA OZELLE studied the fine art of collaborative lithography at Tamarind Institute and became a Tamarind Master Printer in 1992. She has demonstrated her process of waterless lithography at several institutions, including Arizona State University and the University of New Mexico. Ozelle is also an exhibiting artist and is currently preparing for graduate school in her home state of California.

MARK PETR has been a curatorial assistant for prints, drawings, and photographs at the Museum of Fine Arts, Houston, since 1991. Previously, he worked in the prints and drawings collection of the Archer M. Huntington Gallery at the University of Texas at Austin, while completing master's studies in art history, with an emphasis on video art and contemporary critical theory.

STEPHEN PINSON, a recent recipient of the U.S. Department of Education's Jacob K. Javits Fellowship, is currently pursuing graduate studies in art history at the University of Texas at Austin. He formerly worked for Lyons Matrix Gallery, Austin, and served as a curatorial assistant in the print department of the Huntington Art Gallery at the University of Texas, where he participated in numerous exhibitions and specialized in the study of nineteenth-century graphic art. Most recently he contributed the catalogue essay for the Huntington exhibition, *Prints of the Fort Worth Circle 1940–1960*.

JEFFREY RYAN is the owner and director of 21 Steps printmaking workshop in Albuquerque, New Mexico. He catalyzed a broad interest in waterless lithographic print by conducting research and experimentation on the medium at Tamarind Institute between 1987 and 1989. He has since collaborated with about twenty artists on nearly one hundred waterless lithographic editions. He has recently joined the Richard Levy Gallery in Albuquerque to form 21 Steps Editions, publishers and distributors of diverse print editions.

MARY RYAN is the founder, owner, and director of the Mary Ryan Gallery in New York. The gallery, which specializes in American and British works on paper from 1920 through the present, will exhibit works by Eric Avery in the summer of 1994. The Mary Ryan Gallery has published numerous catalogues on American printmakers of the 1930s and 1940s.

ELLEN SRAGOW is director of the Sragow Gallery in New York City. The gallery specializes in American prints, paintings, and works on paper from the 1930s, 1940s, and early 1950s. It also handles American prints from the late 1960s and early 1970s—the New York School. Sragow is a member of the International Fine Print Dealers Association and Art Table, a national organization of professional women in the visual arts.

LINDA TYLER is gallery director at Tamarind Institute and associate editor of *The Tamarind Papers*.

PETER WALCH is director of the University of New Mexico Art Museum, where he has curated numerous exhibitions involving the graphic arts. A former editor of *New Mexico Studies in the Fine Arts* from 1977 through 1987, he writes frequently on European neoclassical art. His will be the lead essay in the forthcoming catalogue of the American Federation of Arts-sponsored touring exhibition, *French Oil Sketches of the Seventeenth, Eighteenth, and Nineteenth Centuries*.

BARRY WALKER, who guest-edits this issue, is curator of prints and drawings at the Museum of Fine Arts, Houston. He was previously with the Brooklyn Museum (1981–1990), where he curated three national print exhibitions as well as solo exhibitions of artists ranging from Goya to Alex Katz. A retrospective of Donald Sultan's prints that he organized is currently touring under the auspices of the American Federation of Arts. He writes frequently on various aspects of contemporary printmaking.

REBA WHITE WILLIAMS and her husband, Dave Williams, who own about 3,500 prints, frequently write about aspects of their collection; the *Burlington Magazine* recently referred to them as "collector-scholars." Mrs. Williams is nearing completion of the doctoral program in art history at the Graduate Center, CUNY. Her article on Robert Gwathmey's prints grew out of her interest in the image of the African-American in prints, an extension of research undertaken for the exhibition *Alone in the Crowd: Prints of the 1930s–1940s by African-American Artists, from the Collection of Reba and Dave Williams.*

PHOTO CREDITS

1.1. Photo by Joe Pineiro, university photographer, Columbia University.

2.1. Edouard Manet, *Guerre civile: scène de la Commune de Paris,* 1871. Courtesy Marion Koogler McNay Art Museum, San Antonio, Texas. Gift of the Friends of the McNay.

2.2. Théodore Géricault, *Le Marechal français,* from *Etudes de chevaux,* 1822. Courtesy the Archer M. Huntington Art Gallery, University of Texas at Austin. Archer M. Huntington Museum Fund, 1992. Photo: George Holmes.

2.3. Bourgeois de la Richardière, *Napoléon, First Consul,* ca. 1802. Courtesy Archer M. Huntington Art Gallery, University of Texas at Austin. Gift of E. Wyllys Andrews IV, 1964. Photo: George Holmes.

2.4. Nicolas-Toussaint Charlet, *French Dragoon with a Flag,* n.d. Courtesy Archer M. Huntington Art Gallery, University of Texas at Austin. Lent by Professor Thomas Bartee, Harvard University. Photo: George Holmes.

2.5. Nicolas-Toussaint Charlet, *Le marchand de dessins lithographique,* 1819. Courtesy Archer M. Huntington Art Gallery, University of Texas at Austin. Purchase as a gift of Marvin Vexler, '48, in memory of Earle Benson, 1989. Photo: George Holmes.

2.6. Honoré Daumier, *Moderne Galilée,* from *La Caricature,* 1834. Courtesy Archer M. Huntington Art Gallery, University of Texas at Austin. Gift of the children of L. M. Tonkin, 1966. Photo: George Holmes.

2.7. Honoré Daumier, *Rue Transnonain, le 15 avril 1834.* Courtesy Marion Koogler McNay Art Museum, San Antonio, Texas. Gift of the Friends of the McNay. Photo: Harvey Patteson & Son.

2.8. Maxime Lalanne, *Démolitions pour le percement de la rue des Ecoles,* n.d. Courtesy Archer M. Huntington Art Gallery, University of Texas at Austin. Archer M. Huntington Museum Fund, 1980. Photo: George Holmes.

2.9. Charles Meryon, *La Morgue,* 1854. Courtesy Archer M. Huntington Art Gallery, University of Texas at Austin. Gift of the children of L. M. Tonkin, 1966. Photo: George Holmes.

3.1-3. American League Against War and Fascism calendar, 1936. Courtesy University Art Museum, University of New Mexico.

4.1. Harry Gottlieb, *Unloading at Majorca,* 1932. Courtesy Sragow Gallery, New York.

4.2. Harry Gottlieb, *Coal Pickers,* 1935–36. Courtesy Sragow Gallery, New York.

4.3. Harry Gottlieb, *Beauticians Academy,* ca. 1936. Courtesy Sragow Gallery, New York.

4.4. Harry Gottlieb, *Bootleg Mining,* 1937. Courtesy Syracuse University Art Collection.

4.5. Harry Gottlieb, *Liberty,* 1941. Courtesy Syracuse University Art Collection.

4.6. Harry Gottlieb, *The Strike Is Won,* 1940. Courtesy Sragow Gallery, New York.

4.7. Portrait of Harry Gottlieb by Amy Gottlieb. Courtesy Amy Gottlieb.

5. All photographs by Dwight Primiano, except the following:

5.5. Robert Gwathmey, *Non-Fiction,* (1945). Courtesy Swann Galleries, Inc., New York.

5.6. Robert Gwathmey, *Singing and Mending,* 1946. Courtesy Butler Institute of American Art, Youngstown, Ohio.

5.7. Robert Gwathmey, *Topping Tobacco,* 1947. Courtesy Butler Institute of American Art, Youngstown, Ohio.

5.8. Robert Gwathmey, *Tobacco Farmers,* 1947. Courtesy Butler Institute of American Art, Youngstown, Ohio.

5.12. Robert Gwathmey, *Farmer's Wife,* 1954. Courtesy Swann Galleries, Inc., New York.

5.17. Robert Gwathmey, *Sharecropper,* (1969). Courtesy Brooklyn Museum.

5.21. Robert Gwathmey, *Hoeing,* (1978). Courtesy Ed Ogul.

6. All Leon Golub and Nancy Spero illustrations, courtesy Josh Baer Gallery, New York; Printworks, Chicago. Photos: David Reynolds.

6.7. Photo: Abe Frajndlich.

7.0. Eric Avery, *Soldiers,* 1992. Courtesy Mary Ryan Gallery. Photo: Adam Reich.

7.1. Eric Avery, *Nuclear Wish for Las Dure Refugee Camp,* 1980. Photo: Roger Haile.

7.2. Eric Avery, *Demoiselles d'Avignon de San Ygnacio,* 1984. Photo: Roger Haile.

7.3. Eric Avery, *Death Gives Birth to Beauty,* 1982. Photo: Roger Haile.

7.4. Eric Avery, *Starving African Child with AIDS*, n.d. Courtesy Eric Avery.

7.5. Eric Avery, *Blood Test,* 1984. Photo: Roger Haile.

7.6. Eric Avery, *U.S.A. Dishonor and Disrespect,* 1990. Printed by Bill Lagattuta at Tamarind Institute. Photo: Damian Andrus.

7.7-10. Eric Avery, *Damn It* suite, 1987. Printed by Bill Lagattuta at Peregrine Press. Photos: Roger Haile.

9.1. Patrick Nagatani, *Katabasis,* 1991. Courtesy Richard Levy Gallery, Albuquerque, New Mexico.

9.2. Patrick Nagatani, *Fin de siècle,* 1989. Courtesy of the artist.

9.3. Patrick Nagatani, *Canandaigua.* Courtesy Richard Levy Gallery, Albuquerque, New Mexico.

10.1-4. All courtesy Richard Levy Gallery, Albuquerque, New Mexico.

11.1-11.9. Photos: Damian Andrus.

11.10. Photo: Jeffrey Sippel.